D1527402

America's
First Indian War

by DENNIS HERRICK

Sterling Publications USA

Kindle Direct Publishing, January 2024

ISBN: 9798425730534

dedicated to BEATRICE

Table of Contents

"We were no match for their numbers, their guns, their cannons. Time in these lands as we knew it was over and we fought the intruders and the terrible weight of knowing with everything in us."

—Joy Harjo, *An American Sunrise*

Prologue

Long before the ocean-to-ocean philosophy of Manifest Destiny, Native Americans resisted their extermination or removal to reservations to make room for settlers—as dictated by that policy.

Their stubborn resistance dates back to the early sixteenth century and lasted for about four hundred years.[i]

European militarism and then US military action and colonist expansion resulted in what at first was gradual and then rapid diminishment of the Indian population in what is now the continental United States.

The resistance spanned four hundred and ten years.[ii] It included battles waged against Juan Ponce de León in 1513, 1517, and 1521. It ended when civilian posses

i

---

[i] Includes all Native American battles, beginning with those in the early sixteenth century. This list includes Spanish expeditions by Juan Ponce de León, who was fatally wounded by a Calusa Indian arrow tipped with poison from Manchineel tree sap; Lucas Vázquez de Allyón, who died trying to colonize Georgia; Pánfilo de Narváez, who was lost in the Gulf of Mexico, and Hernando de Soto, who died from illness near the Mississippi River.

[ii] The *unofficial* US diminishment of Native population includes Spanish expeditions in the early sixteenth century (including slave raids), which cost the lives of many Europeans and Native Americans.

suppressed the "Last Indian Uprising" by Utes and Paiutes in 1923.

Throughout that time, tribes fought against European and then US forces in defense of homelands.

The official US policy maintains that the "Indian Wars" started with the Tiguex War declared and fought in 1540-1541 between Europeans (mostly Spaniards) and the Tiwa tribe of Puebloans in the current state of New Mexico. US policy holds that the "Indian Wars" officially ended with a battle between Yaqui Indians and US Army buffalo soldiers in 1918 in Arizona. Even under the official listing, the Indian Wars spanned three hundred and seventy-seven years.[iii]

Native American resistance included victories, defeats, and stalemate in many battles, intertribal wars, disease, bounties, and slave hunting, which led to inability of tribes to militarily resist any longer.

The Tiguex War started in the winter of 1540–1541 with a declaration of war by Coronado. This book marks the approach of the fifth centenary of the Coronado expedition.

Acknowledgments

Special thanks to Richard and Shirley Cushing Flint, premier historians of the Coronado expedition and authors of several books about the expedition. Also to the late Carroll L. Riley. Cover painting of Coronado expedition is courtesy of Frederic Remington Museum of Art, whose curator, Dr. Laura Desmond, reported that the painting is not copyrighted.

[iii] The *official* US "Indian Wars" record, starts with the Tiguex War in 1540 and ends with the skirmish between Yaqui Indians and the US 10th Cavalry's Buffalo Soldiers in the American Southwest in 1918.

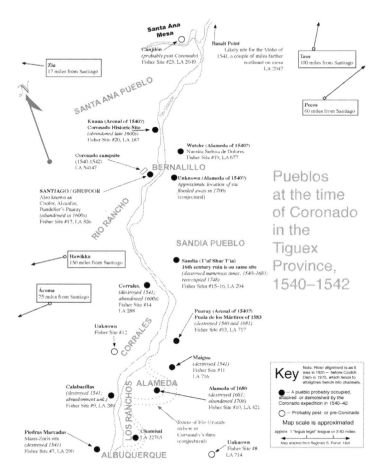

Santa Ana
Mesa

Basalt Point
Likely site for the Moho of
1541, a couple of miles farther
northeast on mesa
LA 2047

Cañjilón
(probably post-Coronado)
Fisher Site #23, LA 2049

Taos
100 miles from Santiago

Zia
17 miles from Santiago

SANTA ANA PUEBLO

Pecos
60 miles from Santiago

Kuaua (Arenal of 1540?)
Coronado Historic Site
(abandoned late 1600s)
Fisher Site #20, LA 187

Watche (Alameda of 1540?)
Nuestra Señora de Dolores
Fisher Site #19, LA 677

Coronado campsite
(1540-1542)
LA 54147

BERNALILLO

Unknown (Alameda of 1540?)
Approximate location of site
flooded away in 1700s
(conjectural)

SANTIAGO / GHUFOOR
Also known as
Coofor, Alcanfor,
Bandelier's Puaray
(abandoned in 1600s)
Fisher Site #17, LA 326

RIO RANCHO

Pueblos
at the time
of Coronado
in the
Tiguex
Province,
1540–1542

SANDIA PUEBLO

Hawikku
150 miles from Santiago

Sandia (T'uf Shur T'ia)
16th century ruin is on same site
(destroyed numerous times, 1540–1681;
reoccupied 1748)
Fisher Sites #15–16, LA 294

Ácoma
75 miles from Santiago

Corrales,
(destroyed 1541;
abandoned 1600s)
Fisher Site #14
LA 288

Puaray (Arenal of 1540?)
Puala de los Mártires of 1583
(destroyed 1540 and 1681)
Fisher Site #13, LA 717

CORRALES

Unknown
Fisher Site #12

Maigua
(destroyed 1541)
Fisher Site #11
LA 716

Calabacillas
(destroyed 1541;
abandonment unk.)
Fisher Site #9, LA 289

LOS RANCHOS

ALAMEDA

Alameda of 1680
(destroyed 1681;
abandoned 1708)
Fisher Site #10, LA 421

Route of Rio Grande
oxbow in
Coronado's time
(conjectural)

Piedras Marcadas
Mann-Zuris site
(destroyed 1541)
Fisher Site #7, LA 290

Chamisal
LA 22765

Unknown
Fisher Site #8
LA 714

ALBUQUERQUE

Key
Note: River alignment is as it
was in 1931 — before Cochiti
Dam in 1975, which tends to
straighten bends into channels.

● — A pueblo probably occupied,
attacked or demolished by the
Coronado expedition in 1540–42

○ — Probably post- or pre-Coronado

Map scale is approximated

approx. 1 "legua legal" league or 2.65 miles

Map adapted from Reginald G. Fisher, 1931

--Map by Dennis Herrick

iii

1 XAUÍAN

History forgot his real name until his Spanish archenemy angrily revealed it inside a jail cell in 1546. Then it was lost again for nearly four hundred years. Finally the Spaniard's deposition was translated into English in a 1940 book, naming the earliest Native American hero: Xauían.[1]

This Pueblo Indian man, whose Tiwa name or part of it is pronounced shah-WEE-on, remains virtually unknown.[2] The reasons are that many historians continue to use his nickname instead of his actual name, and they also tend to downplay or not mention his role in fighting against European invaders.[3]

"European" is used in this book to point out that many of today's nationalities in Europe participated in Spanish expeditions. The Coronado expedition included at least one Englishman, one Scot, four Portuguese, two

---

[1] Hammond and Rey, *Narratives,* Vol II, 359. He still is referred to as Juan Alemán in most history books,

[2] R. Flint. *No Settlement, No Conquest*, 145.

[3] There was no identity as European in the 1500s. The general term was Christians, because Christianity dominated that continent. However, "Christians" was a synonym at that time for Catholics. That eventually changed after Martin Luther's Protestant Reformation in 1517.

Frenchmen, a Belgian, three Italians, two Sicilians, one man from Crete, a German and probably others.[4]

It was the Puebloan man Xauían who led resistance in America's first named Indian war, the Tiguex War, which is so little known that it also needs a pronouncer, TEE-wesh.[5]

The Tiguex War has received little attention despite it being fought 96 years before the Pequot War and 135 years before King Philip's War, both against Native Americans in New England. British colonists landed at Roanoke 45 years after the Tiguex War. British Pilgrims arrived at Plymouth Rock 80 years afterward.

--Adapted from a J.R. Willis postcard of the early 1900s

This adapted picture shows how a two or three-story Rio Grande pueblo such as Xauían's home pueblo of Ghufoor would have appeared as a doorless citadel to Coronado's invasion force of 1540.

---

[4] https://coronado.unm.edu/expedition_members, accessed April 25, 2023.

[5] The Tiguex War was the first named and declared war in which Europeans sought hegemony over a particular tribe and its territory. Thus, the US government recognizes it as the first Indian war for possession of what is now the United States.

Schools for today's students living in the Midwest or populous eastern states rarely teach about early Spanish explorations dating back to the 1500s in New Mexico and Florida—decades before English-speaking peoples arrived on the continent.

Eurocentric accounts of history that do exist immortalized the name of the Spaniard whose expedition invaded New Mexico's Pueblo country in 1540—Coronado.[6] But history has largely ignored Xauían, who defied and fought that Spaniard's expedition.

* * *

An ironic fact is that a team of Spanish horsemen and Mexican Indian allies sent to check the friar's news discredited Friar Marcos de Niza's earlier report about rich cities to the north of New Spain (today's Mexico). If heeded, perhaps the Coronado expedition would not have proceeded. At least, its members and officers would have gone forth with diminished expectations.

A letter sent by Viceroy Antonio de Mendoza y Pacheco to King Carlos I of Spain in 1541 laid out the facts reported by Melchor Díaz—first to Coronado, already en route to the north, and later also by couriers on horses to Mendoza in Mexico City.

Díaz and the fifteen horsemen with him reported that Cíbola (SEE-boh-la) was not a city of wealth as Marcos had reported. Instead it was a village made up of "houses … stone and mud, coarsely worked."

Díaz received his reports on Cíbola from the Indian

---

[6] "Coronado" is an Anglicization of his name. In his day, he would have been known as Francisco Vázquez, not simply as Coronado, the name by which he is best known in the US. However, instead of original z's, Coronado's name often is Anglicized now with either one s or two. Coronado's Spanish name was Francisco Vázquez de Coronado y Luján.

allies he'd sent ahead. The first Indian village in the province they considered to be Cíbola turned out to be the southwestern Zuni pueblo of Hawikku, which Coronado later named as Granada.

Díaz returned to Mexico when he was unable to go forward from the southeastern portion of current Arizona because of cold weather and snow. "They [the Mexican Indian allies sent ahead to Cíbola/Hawikku] were unable to tell me of any metal, nor did they say they [Cíbolans/Zunis] had it." Díaz continued, "They [occupants of Cíbola/Hawikku] have great quantities of turquoise, although not as many as the father provincial [Friar Marcos] said."[7]

This news of no metal wealth and a primitive Native town failed to dissuade Coronado. He already had spent thousands of pesos and borrowed more for the expedition. And Coronado already had started on his way north when Díaz reported to him and later to the viceroy, who also had spent thousands of pesos in equipping, recruiting, and supplying the expedition.

Coronado's expedition had left Culiacán to go north in February 1540 with an advance force of seventy horsemen, thirty men-at-arms on foot, and thousands of Mexican Indian allies. He continued northward despite the discouraging report that Díaz delivered.[8]

---

[7] "Letter from Mendoza to the King, April 17, 1540," reprinted in Castañeda, *Journey of Coronado*, 154-155. Endnotes refer to book of 1904 translated by George Parker Winship. The Spanish king was Carlos I who also ruled with the title of Carlos V (Anglicized to Charles V), as holy Roman emperor. Carlos was the king of Spain (Castile and Aragon then), and he also was the holy Roman emperor, archduke of Austria, lord of the Netherlands, and duke of Burgundy. In effect, Hapsburg royal family members added to his realms.

[8] "*Traslado de las Nuevas*," by anonymous author, reprinted in Castañeda, *Journey of Coronado*. In the more than seventy days from Culiacán to Cíbola, Castañeda reported "some" Negroes and Mexican Indian allies died of hunger or thirst, 163.

The viceroy had conducted recruitment for the expedition. As explained by a 1700s Spanish historian, "The viceroy determined to avail himself of the many noblemen who were in Mexico, who like cork on the water bobbed up and down without having anything to do ... all depending upon the viceroy to do them favors and being maintained at the tables of the citizens of Mexico. Thus it was easy to enlist more than three hundred men, most of them mounted. ... [At Compostela, a small town in the province of Nayarit, Coronado] held a review of the army and found two hundred-seventy mounted men with lances, swords, and other hand weapons, and coats of mail and sallets (helmets) with visors, both of iron and of raw cowhide, and ... seventy infantrymen, both harquebusiers (men armed with arquebus muskets) and others with swords and bucklers (steel shields)."[9]

* * *

Francisco Vázquez de Coronado y Luna was born into a wealthy and politically connected family in Spain. Mendoza as viceroy was the highest ranking Spaniard in Mexico. He was a family friend, and he'd appointed Coronado in his twenties as governor of the Spanish-designated New Galicia Province, northwest of Mexico City. That Spanish province comprises today's Mexican states of Jalisco, Sinaloa, and Nayarit. Coronado controlled some of Mexico's largest estates using Indian forced-labor and slavery. The estates were enormously profitable *encomiendas* given through Coronado's marriage to Beatriz de Estrada in 1537, when she was 12 years old. She was the rich daughter of the former royal treasurer of New Spain (Mexico).

New Galacia was the start of a promising and

---

[9] Day, "Mota Padilla on the Coronado Expedition," 91.

lucrative career. But Coronado gave it up to lead the expedition to the unexplored land Spaniards had come to believe included the "Seven Cities of Cíbola." Those cities were said to be so fabulously wealthy that during the Gold Rush days in California they became popularly known as "Seven Cities of Gold"—although that was an unknown term in the 1500s. Cíbola was a wealthy province of Spanish myth, which Spaniards talked of when referring to what in reality turned out to be the Zuni homeland north of Mexico.

The reasoning for belief in the Seven Cities was that European colonists in Mexico had a Franciscan friar's word that Cíbola was wealthy, like the Aztec city of Tenochtitlán that was demolished and rebuilt as Mexico City. Marcos had reported that Cíbola's first town was as large as Mexico City.

To find out if the friar's reports were true, Coronado's expedition would end up fighting the Zuni, Hopi, Tiwa, and Towa tribes. He also threatened the Tewa and Keres peoples. His main opponents in the war that followed, however, were Tiwa Indians who occupied the middle Rio Grande Valley.

The chronicles referred to the distribution of war prisoners to expedition members as "servants," a euphemism of that time often for forced labor at no pay. Servants sometimes also could refer to paid employees, but there is no indication in the chronicles that the women and children Tiwas captured as prisoners in the Tiguex War were paid.

Many historians have long discounted Coronado's Tiguex War as a mere distraction in an expedition that resulted in Europeans' first sightings of Puebloans, the Rocky Mountains, the Great Plains with its herds of millions of bison, which became better known as buffalo, the Rio Grande, and the attempted exploration of the Grand Canyon.[10]

The Rio Grande has had several names. The first Spaniards to see the river named it the *Rio Nuestra de Señora*, in honor of the Virgin Mary. Later it was known as *Rio Del Norte*, which translates to River of the North. Perhaps because of its rampaging, wandering floods of Coronado's day and colonial years, the Rio Grande reference in Spanish of "Big River" became how it is known today in English.

Accounts of the Tiguex War originated from xenophobic perspectives of *conquistadors*, a Spanish word meaning conquerors. Pedro de Castañeda de Nájera, a horseman on the expedition, wrote about the Tiguex War in only about 40 pages of his translator's 289-page expedition account with related documents.[11] He misunderstood, distorted, or never mentioned much of what happened. Nevertheless, despite its flaws, knowledge of the Coronado expedition would be skeletal without Castañeda's account. Castañeda said he wrote the overall account from memory more than twenty years after the expedition, saying no one else did.

Contemporaneous with Hernando de Soto's raiding

---

[10] Hammond and Rey, *Narratives*, Vol II, 359. It was Cárdenas and his men who first saw the Grand Canyon in the summer or fall of 1540. "It was impossible to descend," Castañeda reported. "The three lightest and most agile men made an attempt to go down at the least difficult place. ... They returned ... not having succeeded in reaching the bottom on account of the great difficulties which they found. ... Those who stayed above had estimated that some huge rocks on the sides of the cliffs seemed to be about as tall as a man, but those who went down swore that when they reached these rocks they were bigger than the great tower of Seville." Castañeda, *Journey of Coronado*, 85-86.

[11] Disregarding front matter and other material, plus an introduction by translator George Parker Winship, the translator added related documents, giving Castañeda's chronicle a total of 289 pages. Although remembered today as Castañeda, he went by the name of Pedro de Castañeda de Nájera. Another Spaniard was to be the expedition's official chronicler, but his report, if he made one, never has been found.

of 1539–1543 through what is now parts of southeast and south central US, Coronado's expedition of 1540-42 was larger. Soto invaded with a mostly all-European force of about seven hundred conquistadors.

Coronado's force included only about three hundred conquistadors, but it also was fortified with an estimated two thousand Mexican Indian allies (*indios amigos*). Coronado also brought thousands of sheep and cattle for food on the hoof as well as hundreds of horses.[12]

Conquest of the joined continental landmasses called the Americas would not have been possible except for conquistadors recruiting large contingents of Mexican Indian allies. In a sense, Spaniards did not conquer the Americas. Indians fighting alongside the Spaniards and killing other Indians made the conquest possible.[13]

Coronado and other Spaniards never referred to Xauían by his Tiwa name in the chronicles. Instead, they called him by the incongruous nickname of Juan Alemán, because they thought he resembled German colonist Juan Henche in Mexico City. (*Alemán* is the Spanish word for German, so Xauían's nickname translates to "John the German.")

If even mentioned at all, history books usually refer to Xauían as Juan Alemán.

This Puebloan leader's Tiwa name might never have come to light if not for Coronado's second-in-command, his *maestre de campo* (literally camp master, but

---

[12] Historian Richard Flint estimates 2,000 Mexican Indians accompanied Coronado. Gerónimo de Zárate Salmerón in his book *Relaciones*, 92-93, reported 2,000 *indios amigos* at Acoma. A Jemez Pueblo kiva mural reportedly portrays visiting Aztecs from Tenochitlán, which by then had been conquered and renamed Mexico City.

[13] Jared Diamond made a similar point in *Guns, Germs, and Steel*, 397. Also Herrick, *Esteban: The African Slave*, 30.

more commonly known as army master or field commander), García López de Cárdenas. His old rank equals a colonel or brigadier general today.

Awaiting trial in Spain for accusations of war crimes at Tiguex, Cárdenas was deposed in his jail cell in 1546. He stated, "An Indian named Xauían ... asked this witness to approach and embrace and seal their peace."[14] Early Spanish chronicles always had identified that Tiwa leader as Juan Alemán.

Cárdenas's deposition is the only mention of Xauían's Tiwa name. Xauían remains the only Puebloan known by his Native name from the Tiguex War.

Xauían should have been a better known figure of American history, as should be the war named for the old Tiguex Province near today's Albuquerque, New Mexico.

Xauían is first in a list of Native American leaders who resisted encroachment of their lands by Europeans, Mexicans, and finally Americans.

Such a list beginning with Xauían includes Po'Pay, Metacomet, Opechancanough, Pontiac, Red Jacket, Tecumseh, Black Hawk, Osceola, Mangas Colorados, Victorio, Cochise, Manuelito, Red Cloud, Crazy Horse, Sitting Bull, Geronimo, Chief Joseph, and many others known and unknown.

Xauían is one of the few with his indigenous name. Most are known by names their enemies called them— such as Pontiac, whose indigenous name was Obwaandi'eyaa.

---

[14] Hammond and Rey, Narratives, Vol II, 359.

2 CLASH OF CIVILIZATIONS

The Albuquerque area's only surviving pueblos where the Southern Tiwa language still is spoken are Sandia and Isleta, although a northern dialect of Tiwa is spoken at Taos and Picuris pueblos north of Santa Fe.

The Keres pueblo of Santa Ana did not exist in its present location in Coronado's time. It was moved later and established near the Jemez River. Similarly, the Keres pueblo of San Felipe did not exist in 1540. It was established along the Rio Grande, inside the former boundaries of Tiguex Province after the war weakened Tiwa rivals. Zia, which still exists, was a Keres pueblo fifteen miles west of the Rio Grande.

Xauían was a leader in the ancient Puebloan religion of kivas and katsinas. The katsinas wore cylindrical head covers and regalia clothing. At Ghufoor Pueblo, Xauían would have been known as a bow chief (war captain) in addition to being a religious leader.

He was born there in the late 1400s into a matrilineal society whose residents lived in walled villages, which Spaniards called pueblos, similar to today's apartment complexes where units are within outside walls.

Spaniards would find Puebloan Indians with the

same basic culture but different languages throughout what would become the state of New Mexico.

Women built and maintained a village's buildings, took care of children, and produced exquisite painted pottery. The pueblos were governed by male religious leaders and members designated as clan leaders. Other men hunted, fished, wove clothes and blankets on looms inside below-ground kivas, and defended the community as warriors. Residents planted, grew, and harvested crops of beans, squash, an early corn called maize, and the world's two great inedibles of tobacco and cotton in their fields irrigated by the Rio Grande.

Unlike Spain's authoritarian leadership, pueblo life was egalitarian with its leaders living in the same pueblo complexes as everyone else.

Ghufoor was a two-story adobe complex, its walls built of dried mud with wood-beam ceilings. Ghufoor was on the west bank of the Rio Grande, across the river from present-day Bernalillo, New Mexico, which is north of today's Albuquerque. The village was located along a trading route that extended from Pecos Pueblo on the edge of the Great Plains westward to Zuni Pueblo, where trade routes continued to Mexico and to the Pacific Ocean.

Ghufoor's Tiwa name translates into English as "parched maize" (corn). Spaniards from Spain's historical region of Castile named the Tiguex Province for the local Tigua (now known as Tiwa) Indians.

Then as now, about five miles to the east a rock and pine-covered colossus loomed across the river nearly a mile above the desert. Northern Puebloans called it "Turtle Mountain," while Tiwas named it *Bien Mur*, meaning simply "Big Mountain." Spaniards would rename it as "Sandia" (Watermelon) Mountain because sunsets often brightened rock on its western cliffside to a red glow.

Dramatic changes occurred in pueblo life when Spaniards first arrived in Coronado's expedition for about two years in 1540. Other Spaniards would come in 1598 to stay for much of the next two hundred years.

Spaniards came from Europe's towering stone-built cathedrals, castles, and sprawling feudal cities ruled by kings and queens in luxurious royalty, whose armies were a dominant military force of Europe.

To Spaniards, the fortified pueblo buildings must have looked like citadels, because there were no doors in the walls but there were loopholes for firing arrows. It was necessary to climb ladders to reach roof levels and then descend other ladders to reach the enclosed rooms. Windows were small and covered with translucent mica.

Eighty percent of Spanish citizens—other than royalty and wealthy landowners—farmed as peasant serfs. Soon upon arrival, Spaniards with horses, guns, armor, lances, and steel swords commandeered the Tiwa pueblo of Ghufoor, which Spaniards pronounced as co-AH-for and transliterated and spelled as Coofor. By 1602, a Spanish map changed the name of the Ghufoor/Coofor site to Santiago Pueblo. The no-longer-existing village's site still is known as Santiago Pueblo.

Spaniards were mystified that Puebloans had no royalty ruling class, such as kings, queens, and dukes, or other noblemen, which they were accustomed to in Europe. Expedition Captain Hernando de Alvarado wrote of this contrast with Europe's rulers that surprised expedition members. "Those who have the most authority among [Puebloans]," he wrote, "are the old men. We regarded them as witches."[1]

---

[1] "Narrative of Alvarado" reprinted in *Journey of Coronado,* 243.

In contrast to Spaniards' Christian Catholicism, the Puebloans' ancient religion included kiva rooms dug eight to ten feet deep. Ceremonial dances in the plazas featured katsinas, where men put on cylindrical head covers and wore regalia specific to the spirit represented.[2]

This book's author carved, painted, and clothed this four-inch figure as an approximation of the Chákwaina katsina, named for Esteban, the African slave from Morocco who was the first non-Indian to find Zuni in 1539. This figure is not authentic because it was created by a non-Puebloan. It's intended to give an idea of a katsina without a photograph of one, which some Puebloans would consider sacrilegious. Most modern Cháikwaina katsina head covers include a crescent moon and star to symbolize Esteban's Muslim heritage in Morocco.

Each katsina (Anglicized as kachina) represented personification of spirits that would take people's prayers to the Creator and instruct Puebloans on how to live. Men felt spiritually ennobled when wearing the regalia and a head cover of a katsina—much like Spaniards' own Catholic clergy and other church leaders

---

[2] The photo of a katsina figure carving represents the Moroccan slave Esteban, who was remembered by Pueblo Indians because he was a prelude of the disruption to their society when Europeans arrived the next year. The Islamic Center of Washington, DC, honors Esteban as the first Muslim to enter what is now the United States. See *Esteban: The African Slave*, a historical biography, 4-5. Also, Paul Coze, "Kachinas: Masked Dancers." Three early depictions of historic katsinas can be seen as painted in a Zuni church in Halona in the book by Daniel Gibson, *Pueblos of the Rio Grande*, 96–97.

do when they wear their religious vestments.

However, the appearance of katsinas seemed bizarre to sixteenth century Christians. Thus, katsinas wearing full head covers ("masks" as the Spaniards called them) led Franciscan friars with Coronado's expedition to consider katsinas to be representations of the devil. This impression of the friars led Catholic Spaniards to think that Indians were devil-worshippers. Many, if not most, thought that Indians were sub-humans.

There were a reported twelve Tiguex Province villages.[3] They were situated along about thirteen miles on both sides of the Rio Grande from Isleta Pueblo, which still exists today, north at least to Kuaua Pueblo, home of the Coronado Historic Site, and even beyond. Spaniards reported other tribes of Puebloans had built villages north and south along the banks of the Rio Grande or at a distance to the east and west. Tribes of Puebloans living in other villages were described as having similar cultures to the Tiguex Province.

* * *

Viceroy Mendoza might have been motivated to authorize the expedition in part by Franciscan Friar Marcos's false report that he had seen riches at the purported Seven Cities in 1539. It was later learned that Marcos's African guide Esteban reached the first encountered Cíbola village of Hawikku, but Marcos was

---

[3] The historic-era pueblos of Tiguex Province at the time of contact from north to generally south with their modern names are: Kuaua, Watche, Alameda, Santiago, Corrales, Sandia, Puaray, Maigua, Calabacillas, Chamisal, Piedras Marcadas, and Isleta. A pueblo, perhaps named Alameda, lay between Watche and Sandia and it might have been destroyed by a 1700s flood in or near the current town of Bernalillo, New Mexico. A second pueblo also named Alameda did not exist in Coronado's time, and its site later became Alameda Elementary School. Only Sandia and Isleta still exist as Tiwa pueblos in the old Tiguex Province. A partially restored Kuaua Pueblo is at Coronado Historic Site.

hundreds of miles behind Esteban. His unfamiliarity with the route upon entering the present states of Arizona and New Mexico accounted for his disorientation guiding the Coronado expedition a year later. His confusion cost some expeditionaries their lives from hunger or thirst.

Esteban's success in reaching the Zuni Pueblo of Hawikku caused Zuni historian Joe S. Sando to remark, "The first white man our people saw was a Black man."[4]

An advance force of conquistadors and Mexican Indian allies guided by Friar Marcos were the first Coronado expedition members to appear at Cíbola/Hawikku the following year, in the summer of 1540.

Castañeda wrote about expedition members' sighting of the first village, which was then called by the name of the purported province, Cíbola, although it was the Hawikku Pueblo of Zuni Indians. He wrote, "When they saw the first village … such were the curses that some hurled at Friar Marcos that I pray God may protect him from them." Marcos had never seen Cíbola/Hawikku although he'd reported it was a rich Indian town bigger than Mexico City.

Castañeda described Hawikku as "a little, crowded village, looking as if it had been crumpled all up together. There are ranch houses in New Spain [Mexico] which make a better appearance at a distance. It is a village of about 200 warriors, is three and four stories high, with the houses [apartment rooms] small."[5]

Although the Tiguex War would not start until

---

[4] Sando, *Pueblo Nations*, 50.

[5] Castañeda, *Journey of Coronado*, 23. This book includes selected excepts of Castañeda and other writers about the Coronado expedition, but a complete online facsimile of Castañeda's account is available at https://www.americanjourneys.org/aj-086/

December, the expedition's first battle occurred in July 1540 at Cíbola/Hawikku in New Mexico. Spanish horseman Castañeda reported "These folk waited for the army.[6] ... The city was deserted by men over 60 years and under 20 at Hawikku" when expeditionaries arrived.[7] When [the Zunis] refused to have peace on the terms the interpreters extended ... they were at once put to flight." Coronado and his advance force charged after a Zuni priest sprinkled a line of cornmeal and said they should not cross it. In a letter to Viceroy Mendoza a month after the battle, Coronado reported how he led the attack in his gold-plated armor. But he was injured when knocked down by Indians throwing large rocks while he was climbing a ladder set as a trap against a wall.[8]

Cárdenas and Hernando de Alvarado threw their armored bodies over Coronado, probably saving his life.

Expeditionaries drew back because of the accuracy of Zuni arrows fired from the rooftops. The *Relación del Succeso* reported, "We began to assault them from a distance with the artillery and musket fire, and that afternoon they surrendered."

Coronado sent a letter to the viceroy in August 1540 after the Hawikku battle. He reported, "[Friar Marcos]

---

6 Castañeda often used the word "army" to refer to the Coronado expedition. However, few members had military experience. The expedition consisted of colonists and hidalgos recruited in Mexico. Castañeda, *Journey of Coronado*, 23-24.

7 The Zuni homeland includes part of today's Cibola County in New Mexico. Coronado named the first village of Hawikku as Granada. "Traslado de las Nuevas," reprinted in Castañeda, *Journey of Coronado*, 163.

8 "The Nominal Target of the Investigation," R. Flint, *Great Cruelties*, 281. Coronado apparently was seriously injured and carried unconscious from the battle with a head injury and arrow wounds. He never again personally led an attack against Puebloan warriors.

has not told the truth in a single thing that he said." Coronado decided he must seek riches elsewhere because of the friar's deception. Coronado reassured the viceroy in a letter, "It does not appear to me that there is any hope of getting gold or silver (at Cíbola), but I trust in God that, if there is any, we shall get our share of it, and it shall not escape us through any lack of diligence in the search."[9]

* * *

In ordering Coronado northward, Viceroy Mendoza might have been at least in part motivated by Franciscan Friar Marcos's false report that Marcos had seen riches at the first of the Seven Cities. At first, Mendoza was thinking of leading the expedition, but he didn't.

A lead element of Coronado's expedition converged on Ghufoor Pueblo to the east several weeks after attacks against Zunis at Hawikku Pueblo and a Hopi village farther west.

Even before Spaniards arrived at Ghufoor on the west bank of the Rio Grande, runners had told Puebloans that Spaniards had attacked Zuni and Hopi Puebloans.

* * *

Coronado ordered Captain Hernando Alvarado to take a force east from Hawikku to investigate stories they'd heard about a large river, irrigated Indian crop fields, and a vast prairie where the huge herds of buffalo roamed.

Alvarado led the exploratory group of twenty

---

[9] "Translation of a Letter from Coronado to Mendoza, August 3, 1540," reprinted in Castañeda, *Journey of Coronado*, 183. It reveals how Coronado changed his expedition mission to finding gold and silver instead of the original mission of finding a land route to the wealth of China and Greater India. The letter was written a month after the battle because it took that long for Coronado to recover from his wounds at Hawikku.

conquistadors and an unknown number of Mexican Indian allies to what the Spaniards would name the Tiguex Province. He arrived in September 1540 at Ghufoor Pueblo, where a trading route crossed the Rio Grande from east to west.

Alvarado's advance force included an Indian trader from Pecos Pueblo, called Bigotes, whom the Spaniards are said to have nick-named as "Whiskers." (A mistranslation, because the Spanish word *bigotes* more properly means mustache on a human.)[10] The trader's mustache was unusual for an Indian of the time. A description exists that he had a "long mustache." He probably was taller than most Indians or Europeans, and had the muscled physique of an athlete. Castañeda must have been impressed in his description of Bigotes: "He was a tall, well-built young fellow, with a fine figure."[11] Bigotes probably was not his Indian name.

The well-known Pecos man's presence reassured Tiwas about the strangers. However, Xauían realized the Spaniards—which the Indians referred to as "metal people" because of their weapons and armor—were warlike. He knew of their attacks against fellow Puebloans at the Zuni and Hopi villages. At first,

---

[10] Castañeda, *Journey of Coronado*, 38. The best translation for an English reader of Castañeda's Spanish word of *bigotes* is "mustache." (Although bigotes in Spanish could translate to "whiskers," as cited by Castañeda on pages 38, 44, 47, 61, and 64, George Parker Winship's translation of the word is for whiskers on, for example, a cat.) Winship's translation does not capture the English equivalency of "mustache," which would result in the Pecos trader being known as "Captain Whiskers" for the next century. Richard Flint and Shirley Cushing Flint clarified the 16th-century word as being intended to mean a prominent mustache in their *Documents* in 2012.

[11] Castañeda's description of Bigotes was the only description of personal appearance for anyone on the expedition. Castañeda, *Journey of Coronado*, 38.

Xauían had Tiwas of other Tiguex villages come to Ghufoor and welcome the bearded strangers.

Vastly outnumbered, with only fifty or so warriors in a typical Tiwa village, Xauían tried at first to avoid a confrontation.

Hoping to avoid the fate of Zuni and Hopi, Xauían had Indians from Tiguex villages bring food, buffalo robes, turquoises, and trade items to Ghufoor with a musical welcome played for the bearded Spaniards and their Mexican Indian allies on drums, flutes, and gourd rattles.[12]

Unknown to Xauían and the other Tiguex Tiwas, Alvarado considered the welcome as meaning Puebloans would support the expedition with food and supplies and that they were more like laborers than warriors."[13] The Spanish chronicler Castañeda would later write, "Alvarado sent messengers back [to Hawikku] to advise the general to come and winter in [the Tiguex Province]." However, Coronado testified in the later investigation on charges of war crimes that the invitation to go to Tiguex was sent by Friar Juan de Padilla, a Franciscan missionary traveling with Alvarado. Regardless, Castañeda wrote, "The general was not a little relieved to hear that the country was growing better."

After his Ghufoor welcome, Alvarado left to travel farther east to see the "cows" (buffalo herds) that Indians had reported as innumerable and roamed a large grassy plain.

Alvarado traveled with Turk, a Pawnee Indian guide

---

[12] Ibid., 40.

[13] An important (and mistaken) description of Puebloans, which Castañeda offered to Spaniards hoping to use Indian slave labor on any encomiendas they might establish on the expedition.

living at Pecos Pueblo, into the Great Plains. Using European logic, Alvarado concluded Turk was a Pecos slave, but Turk's independence indicates otherwise. Castañeda reported, "They called the Indian Turk, because he looked like one." Cloth wrapped around the Pawnee's head made him appear like the Spaniards' Ottoman Empire enemies from Turkey who wore turbans.

Castañeda wrote that Turk told Alvarado, "there were large settlements in the farther part of that country … [Turk] told [Alvarado and his men] so many and such great things about the wealth of gold and silver in his country that they did not care about looking for cows, but returned [to Hawikku] after they had seen some few, to report the rich news to the general."

Meanwhile, disappointed that the Seven Cities of Cíbola were only stone and dried mud adobe villages of Zuni Indians, Coronado made plans to relocate. Alvarado's report back to him sounded like Alvarado had found a village farther east beside a river that was more promising. Spaniards would end up considering what they named Tiguex Province as the heart of pueblo country.

Coronado had remained with much of his advance force of conquistadors and Mexican Indian allies among the emptied Zuni pueblos, which the Natives abandoned after the Hawikku battle and went to the top of Dowa Yalanne mesa. He'd sent Alvarado and other conquistadors out to explore the countryside, which resulted in other expeditionaries finding the Hopi villages and Grand Canyon.

Spaniards had let Zuni defenders of Hawikku escape by letting them leave the pueblo when Indian defense turned hopeless.

Stranded in otherwise empty Zuni country,

Coronado ordered his second-in-command Cárdenas to go to where Alvarado had found Ghufoor Pueblo to find lodging for the expedition in that area. The rest of the expedition was at that time in conquered Hawikku. So Cárdenas perhaps assumed that Coronado meant Cárdenas must conquer a different pueblo in the part of the country where Alvarado had gone. Maybe Coronado ordered Cárdenas to do so. No clear motive for Cárdenas later assaulting Ghufoor is in the chronicles.

Soon Cárdenas arrived at Ghufoor with a large force of conquistadors and Mexican Indian allies. Seeing the weather becoming colder and snowier, Cárdenas decided better shelter was needed than the expedition's tents. He put his sights on Ghufoor village. Time was running out because Cárdenas knew Coronado would soon arrive. So Cárdenas issued an ultimatum that Tiwas must leave Ghufoor so the expedition could move in.

Puebloan leaders discussed in a meeting inside their underground kiva what their response should be to the Spanish demand that they leave Ghufoor. Despite having greeted Alvarado's men just a few weeks earlier in friendship, the strangers now insisted that Tiwas needed to abandon Ghufoor.

Resistance was born in that kiva meeting. Xauían went to Cárdenas and told him that the Tiwas could not leave their homes, their crop fields, and the graves of their ancestors.

The Spanish mindset of the time was to not negotiate with Indians, who were to obey or suffer the consequences.

Cárdenas's force attacked Ghufoor to evict its Tiwa occupants. Despite Spanish accounts implying the Indians turned over the pueblo voluntarily, archaeologists at Ghufoor's site in 1934 found fired arquebus musket balls and crossbow points, proving an

21

unreported battle took place.[14] They also found a Tiwa warrior's skeleton in a Ghufoor room with a crossbow point inside the rib cage—America's earliest verified victim of European warfare against Native Americans.[15]

Cárdenas's force of conquistadors and Mexican Indian allies attacked Ghufoor to evict the Tiwa occupants. He sent an unknown number, probably in the hundreds, of Mexican Indian allies, in the attack against Ghufoor Pueblo. Although their total was never reported, historian Richard Flint wrote the Indian allies included ferocious Aztecs, Tlatelolcas, Tarascos and other Mexican Indian warriors. The reputation for relishing combat of the estimated two thousand Mexican Indian warriors on the expedition might have intimidated many Puebloans.[16]

As bow chief and war captain, Xauían would have led the defense against an overwhelming attack against Ghufoor.

Castañeda wrote, "As it was necessary that the

---

[14] Vierra. "A Sixteenth Century Campsite," 4-13. The arquebus was a matchlock, muzzle-loading, smoothbore musket. Its long, iron barrel was so heavy that it was propped on a forked pole when firing. The Spanish word was *arcabuz*. The expedition had twenty-one arquebuses and nineteen crossbows. Coronado was the only European to bring crossbows to what became the US Southwest. The expedition's power included horses. Castañeda noted that horses "frighten the enemy most." Castañeda, *Journey of Coronado*, 147.

[15] Tichy. "The Archaeology of Puaray," 145–146. Some of 1934's excavators of Ghufoor Pueblo, now known as Santiago, thought the west side river site was "Puaray" or "Bandelier's Puaray," but most decided Puaray Pueblo was on the east side of the Rio Grande. Tichy at first thought the crossbow point might be the point of a quill.

[16] A number of Mexican Indian allies joined in the attack against Ghufoor. Castañeda rarely made mention of Mexican Indian allies, even though they made up four-fifths of the expedition. Many Mexican Indians were recruited by assuring them they could take captive Puebloan warriors back to Mexico for sacrifice to the gods of Mexican allies. Also, R. Flint, "Without Them, Nothing was Possible."

natives should give the Spaniards lodging places, the people in one village [Ghufoor] had to abandon it and go to others belonging to their friends, and they took with them nothing but themselves and the clothes they had on." An expedition member noted, "The people of Tiguex did not feel well about this seizure."[17]

On Coronado's way to Tiguex, the freezing winter of 1540-41 began to cover what is now the state of New Mexico with snow and ice. It was a severe winter compared with present-day weather because much of North America was then in the Little Ice Age.

Castañeda experienced the worsening winter weather as Coronado's force traveled from Hawikku through the central part of today's New Mexico. Struggling to find their way in constant snowstorms, Castañeda reported that one night was especially brutal, writing, "Snow fell all night long … so that if any one had suddenly come upon the army nothing would have been seen but mountains of snow. The horses stood half buried in it."[18]

Cárdenas's attack drove the Tiwas out of Ghufoor Pueblo while Coronado was on his way from Hawikku with more of the expedition.

Castañeda's only mention of an attack on Ghufoor was, "Our men had also burnt a village the day before the army arrived."

* * *

The 29-or-30-year-old Coronado realized tension between Tiwas and the expedition as soon as he arrived in the Tiguex Province in December 1540. That's when

---

[17] "Juan de Contreras, Fifth *de Oficio* Witness." Richard Flint, *Great Cruelties*, 112.

[18] Castañeda, *Journey of Coronado*, 46. This page also was where Castañeda's comment appeared about burning a village the day before Coronado arrived.

Cárdenas informed Coronado that he had commandeered Ghufoor Pueblo for the expedition's headquarters on the day before Coronado arrived.

Shortly after Coronado's arrival, Alvarado returned from the Great Plains and introduced the Pawnee Turk to Coronado, saying Turk had accused Bigotes of taking a gold armband (or bracelets) from him. Alvarado told Coronado about Turk's description of his country, called Quivira (kee-VIR-ah). Castañeda reported, "The Turk told that in his country there was a river in the level country ... in which there were fishes as big as horses, and large numbers of very big canoes, with more than twenty rowers on a side, and that they carried sails, and that their lords sat ... under awnings. ... He said also that the lord of that country took his afternoon nap under a great tree on which were hung a great number of little gold bells, which put him to sleep as they swung in the air. He said also ... the jugs and bowls were of gold. He called gold acochis." Castañeda wrote that Turk said his Pawnee country was near a river much larger than even the Rio Grande just outside Coronado's Ghufoor walls. The larger river is known today as the Mississippi River. "For the present, [Turk] was believed."[19]

Coronado was heartened by Alvarado's news that gold articles and quantities of gold might finally be within his grasp.

European lust for gold pushed all other expedition

---

[19] Ibid., 43, 81. Spaniards, like American prospectors centuries later and lottery buyers today, seemed to believe anything if there was a prospect for quick riches. Fish as big as horses were true, because at that time the Mississippi River had huge sturgeon fish and even bull sharks. The canoes and rulers were Turk's description of the Mississippian Culture, that flourished for hundreds of years after 800. Turk's rumors of gold were untrue—or mistaken. The possibility of attaining gold was to lure the expedition away from Tiguex Province.

objectives aside. Viceroy Mendoza had sent Coronado north to find a northern land route to Asia and its luxuries of silk, spices, porcelains, dyes, and other valuable goods. The thinking of the time was that a land route to Greater India and China existed north or even west of Mexico.

But Coronado had become determined to make the expedition profitable for its many investors, who included himself, the viceroy, and even several expeditionaries.

After hearing Turk's exciting gold news, one of Coronado's first decisions was to send Alvarado back to Pecos Pueblo to learn more about any gold armbands that Turk had said Bigotes had taken from him. Coronado thought Pecos leaders could tell him more about the gold. He didn't realize that Puebloan Indians were not familiar at that time with the metal. He also decided to travel farther east to the Turk's country of Quivira. He hoped to find gold and silver there, and also dense populations where Spaniards could establish encomienda estates with Indian forced labor and tribute payments.

Upon returning to Pecos, Alvarado saw no other means to obtain information about gold armbands, so he tricked the trader Bigotes and an "old man" from Pecos whom Castañeda called the pueblo's governor. Castañeda perhaps misidentified the elderly Pecos man as the governor. The aged man might have been the pueblo's religious leader known as a cacique. Alvarado invited the two Pecos men to his tent as well as Plains Indians Ysopete and Turk. Then he bound them with collars and chains to take back as prisoners to Coronado at Ghufoor/Coofor. Castañeda reported that when "that province sent messengers [asking that] the four Indians be given back ... Alvarado unleashed Spanish war dogs on the messengers, who were bitten badly."

Castañeda concluded, "This began the want of confidence in the word of the Spaniards whenever there was talk of peace from this time on, as will be seen by what happened afterward."[20]

The Pecos leaders were interrogated for several months and tortured. Under Spanish law, torture was permitted during interrogation, and expedition members would subject other Indians to torture under questioning. Spaniards sicced war dogs on Bigotes at least once. The dogs bit Bigotes on the arms and legs in vain attempts by Spaniards to get information about gold. Bigotes and the elderly Pecos captive insisted gold armbands didn't exist and that Turk was lying.

Xauían met frequently with Coronado after the Ghufoor battle. Although then a refugee from Ghufoor, he tried to smooth relations between Tiwas and the expedition. Negotiations ended when Coronado demanded that Xauían order Tiwa villages to turn over buffalo robes and blankets to warm expedition members in winter conditions. Both Spaniards and their Mexican Indian allies came from "ever lasting summer" areas in Mexico, and some had frozen to death.

Castañeda wrote, "[Coronado] summoned one of the chief Indians of Tiguex, a principal of Tiguex with whom he was already well acquainted, and had already had much intercourse and with whom he was on good terms." Castañeda wrote that the Indian "was called Juan Alemán by our men, after a Juan gentleman who lived in Mexico, whom he was said to resemble." Castañeda reported, "The general told this man [Xauían] that he must furnish about three hundred or

---

20 Ibid., 44. Also see, "Juan de Contreras, Fifth *de Oficio* Witness." R. Flint, *Great Cruelties*, 112.

more pieces of cloth, which he needed to give his people."

On one side of this meeting was the slave-owning, bearded, rich, and young Spanish general wearing the finest clothes that sixteenth-century money could buy. Facing him was a bronze-skinned and smooth-faced older man from an egalitarian society who wore moccasins, deerskin leggings, a cotton shirt, and a buffalo robe because of a cold and snowy winter.

* * *

The original plan had been for three ships captained by Hernando de Alarcón to resupply Coronado's expedition with food and winter clothing. Alarcón had sailed up the southern end of the Colorado River from present-day Yuma, Arizona, at the Gulf of California, known at that time as the Sea of Cortés. But Alarcón realized the distance across desert to reach Coronado was too vast. He and his ships returned to Mexico. Alarcón is virtually unique among sixteenth century conquistadors because he treated Indians that he met benevolently.[21]

Xauían told Coronado that he could not provide the warmer clothing that Coronado demanded. Castañeda wrote that (Xauían) said, "It pertained to the governors, and that besides this they would have to consult together and divide it among the villages, and that it was necessary to make the demand of each town separately."[22]

Castañeda reported that expedition members

---

[21] Because Alarcón treated Indians fairly and humanely, Bernard de Voto, in his *Westward the Course of Empire*, observed, "The Indians had an experience they were never to repeat: they were sorry to see these white men leave."

[22] "Castañeda de Nájera's Narrative," Flint and Flint. *Documents,* 402. Also, Castañeda, *Journey of Coronado,* 46-47.

responded to Xauían's refusal by going to pueblos and seizing what they wanted. They often stripped blankets and buffalo robes off Tiwa elders and women. In his typical understated manner, Castañeda wrote that these confiscations "caused not a little hard feeling."[23]

During these assaults for warmer clothing, a Puebloan man reported that a Spaniard raped his mate at a pueblo called *Arenal*, a Spanish or Castilian word referring to sand. That name could apply to most Tiguex desert pueblos. Arenal Pueblo's original name is unknown. Historians believe it was either Puaray Pueblo on the east side of the Rio Grande about three miles south of present-day Sandia Pueblo, or else at Kuaua Pueblo, about two miles northeast of Ghufoor/Coofor on the river's west bank.[24] Other rapes are implied during the expedition's proximity to pueblo villages.

Francisca de Hozes, a Spanish woman on the expedition, said the Indians rebelled "because their wives, daughters, and other things they had in their houses were taken by force and against their will."[25]

Historian Paul Schneider observed in his book *Brutal Journey*, "It was not a fortunate thing to be a young woman in a village" near a Spanish expedition encampment.

The Arenal woman's outraged mate went to now-occupied Ghufoor/Coofor with his village's leaders to

---

[23] Castañeda, *Journey of Coronado*, 48.

[24] Arenal's Tiwa name and location remain uncertain. Spaniards at one time called that large pueblo Puaray, or Puala. Later it was referred to as *pueblo del mártires.* Surface artifacts have been collected, but the presumed site never has been excavated because it has been covered with housing for decades.

[25] "*First de Officio* Witness," R. Flint, *Great Cruelties,* 58.

complain. The rapist presumably was Juan de Villegas.[26] He never was punished. Some expeditionaries speculated that because Villegas's brother was a member of Mexico City's governing council, Coronado and his officers looked the other way.

The woman's mate could not identify Villegas. Perhaps Villegas changed his clothes, or all bearded Spaniards looked alike to him. But the woman's mate identified Villegas's peach-colored horse because he'd held the bridle of the man's horse while the man climbed a ladder to rooftop entrances to pueblo rooms. Coronado refused to believe the man and sent him away "without any satisfaction."[27]

Tiwas already were desperate because expeditionaries took their food and clothing in December. They possibly were upset further because of Mexican Indian allies picking fights with Tiwas because they were permitted to take captives as a privilege given by Spaniards for joining the expedition. Tiwas also were angry because Spaniards let horses graze in hundreds of acres of harvested Indian cornfields. With wood scarce except at miles away in the mountains, Puebloans relied on cornstalks for winter fuel. They considered grazing animals endangering that resource. They didn't realize animals could graze in harvested fields in Europe.

Castañeda reported: "The next day one of the [Mexican] Indians, who was guarding the horses of the army, ran to [Ghufoor/Coofor] saying the Indians were driving off the horses toward their villages. Estimates were that thirty to sixty horses, mules, and pack animals

---

[26] R. Flint, *No Settlement, No Conquest*, 147. Also, "The Nominal Target of the Investigation, Francisco Vázquez de Coronado," in R. Flint, *Great Cruelties*, 287.

[27] Castañeda, *Journey of Coronado*, 49.

were killed. The Spaniards tried to collect the horses again, but many were lost, besides seven of the general's mules."[28]

It is believed that Spaniards by then occupied two pueblos—Ghufoor and possibly a vacant pueblo the Spaniards named Alameda in or near what would become Bernalillo, New Mexico. That pueblo might have been the village demolished two centuries later by a Rio Grande flood. (A subsequent pueblo also was named Alameda in what would become northern Albuquerque.)

Coronado convened a *junta*, a meeting of Franciscan friars with the expedition, royal officials, captains, and other notable persons. The decision was that the Tiwas' theft and killing of horses and mules was an act of war.[29] Coronado then ordered retaliation with no quarter to be given—the Tiguex War.

* * *

The friars' permission at the junta was vital in Coronado's decision to declare the Tiguex War. Soon the cultivated country along the Rio Grande erupted with a bloody war in the first winter of 1540–41, devastating the Tiguex Province's farming pueblos.

Viceroy Mendoza had ordered Coronado to treat Indians benevolently. The viceroy had received a letter five years earlier from Spanish King Carlos I, who'd written: "The murder, plundering, and other improper

---

[28] Estimates of horses, mules, and pack animals killed varied. The " *Relación del Suceso*" reported forty horses and mules were killed. It is believed The *Relación* was written by Coronado's scribe, Hernando Bermejo. Castañeda, *Journey of Coronado*, 199.

[29] "Everyone [at the *junta*, including the friars] jointly determined that war should be waged against the Indians of that province and that they should be punished," in "Diego López, Second *de Parte* Witness," R. Flint, *Great Cruelties*, 393. See also "Further Defense" in *Great Cruelties*, 440.

acts that have been done in the said conquest, as well as capturing Indians as slaves, should cease."

Pope Paul III in 1537 issued his *Sublimis Deus* papal bull, declaring that Indians were humans with souls and should be treated humanely and not enslaved.[30]

Coronado had promised Mendoza that he would adhere to the viceroy's instruction on treating Indians he met with patience and good will. But he had already broken that promise by hanging several Indian men and women on the way through Mexico for living in an area where an Indian archer had killed an expeditionary. Then he'd led a sudden attack against the Zunis, with his horsemen lancing several Zunis fleeing across an open plain and his expedition assaulting the pueblo where they lived. After that, members of his expedition had charged and killed Hopi warriors who, like the Zuni priest at Hawikku, had refused them entry.

In the Tiguex Province, hundreds of Tiwa warriors would die in battles with Coronado's force of Europeans and Mexican Indian allies during the Tiguex War of 1540–41, followed by guerrilla warfare in the second winter of 1541–42.

Hundreds of women and children would be taken prisoner to serve as "servants" to expedition members. Coronado later would take his prisoners with his expedition onto the Great Plains. Then he proceeded with an advance force across the Great Plains to find Quivira, which would turn out to be toward the northern middle of the present state of Kansas.

Another long-running consequence from conquering Hawikku was that Zunis banned Hispanics from attending their public feast day dances into the

---

[30] R. Flint, *Great Cruelties*, 1, on the king's order. For information on the papal bull, go online to see en.wikipedia.org/wiki/Sublimis_Deus.

twentieth century because Coronado's expeditionaries broke apart wooden Zuni altars for firewood.[31]

Coronado's expeditionaries had arrived in 1540 wearing "armor made of steel or many layers of leather, and they carried swords and terrifying guns," while Puebloans "were armed only with stone weapons," reported historian Franklin Folsom.[32] "So it was easy for Coronado to force them to feed [his expedition members] and his horses. ... The [Europeans] took not only food from their villages, but freedom, too" in dispossession, warfare fatalities, and forced labor.

Folsom wrote that Coronado's expedition came "seeking" gold and other precious metals." However, the original mission had been to find a route to Far East wealth. Coronado changed the mission to a search for Quivira riches after disappointing poverty by European standards of the mythical "Seven Cities."

For disobeying his king, his immediate superior the viceroy, and the pope on issues of slavery, and his failure to find northern riches, plus deciding to leave the Indians at war by returning without orders, Francisco Vázquez de Coronado would be called to a legal accounting as no ruthless conquistador before him ever had been.

---

[31] Simmons. "Coronado blunder," A-8.

[32] Folsom. *Red Power*, 43.

3 RESISTANCE

"Santiago!" was the conquistadors' battle cry. In English, the battle cry means "St. James and at them!" Was Ghufoor/Coofor eventually renamed Santiago Pueblo on a 1602 map based on the battle cry, or was it named after St. James, the patron saint of conquistadors? Regardless, that word would be a fitting name for the luckless pueblo from which Coronado launched his attacks against the rest of the Tiguex Province in the winter of 1540–41. A phase of the war continued the following winter with the expedition struggling against Tiwa guerrilla warfare.

Because the Tiwas killed horses, mules, and pack animals in 1540, Coronado ordered Cárdenas to go with a force to Arenal where several animals had been taken.[1]

At Arenal, where the rape had been reported, Cárdenas found the pueblo's entrances barricaded with logs. A "great noise" came from inside the pueblo where horses were being chased and shot with arrows.

The expedition's hundreds of Spaniards and Mexican Indians surrounded Arenal and made ready to attack. Two elderly Puebloans emerged and walked

---

[1] The attack against Arenal was the first battle of the Tiguex War.

without weapons toward the Spaniards for negotiation, but Spanish horsemen lanced them from behind before they could meet with Cárdenas.[2]

For two days conquistadors attacked Arenal, using scaling ladders against the doorless walls. The expeditionaries attacked with arquebus muskets, crossbows, swords, and a horde of Mexican Indian allies. The Tiwa defense caused many casualties and delayed the expeditionaries from reaching Arenal's rooftops. According to Castañeda, the Europeans and Mexican Indian allies eventually reached the roof. Through holes the next day into the rooms, they tossed in burning brush, smoking out the Arenal defenders, "who begged for peace."

Castañeda reported that Pablo de Melgosa and Diego López were on Arenal's roof. Indians made crosses, which were a sign of peace for Puebloans. The expeditionaries responded by making the sign of a cross with their hands. "[The Tiwas] then put down their arms and received pardon. They were taken to [Cárdenas's large and brightly colored field tent]."

Melchior Pérez testified that Cárdenas promised Arenal's defenders that they would be guaranteed safety if they surrendered. Pérez testified he said to Cárdenas, "Lord, do not [make the sign of the cross to urge Tiwas to surrender] unless you expect to fulfill [your promise]." Pérez said that Cárdenas replied, "He had had made the [sign of the cross] incorrectly."[3]

Castañeda wrote about what happened next. "As [Cárdenas] had been ordered by [Coronado] not to take

---

[2] "Juan de Troyano, Eighth *de Oficio* Witness." R. Flint, *Great Cruelties*, 176.

[3] "Melchior Pérez, Tenth *de Oficio* Witness." R. Flint, *Great Cruelties,* 216. By coincidence, making the motion of a cross was a sign of peace to both Puebloans and Spaniards.

them alive, but to make an example of them so that the other natives would fear the expedition, [Cárdenas] ordered two hundred stakes to be prepared at once to burn them alive."[4]

He continued, "When the [Tiwas in the tent] saw that the Spaniards were binding and beginning to roast [about thirty to fifty warriors], about a hundred men who were in the tent began to struggle and defend themselves with what there was there and with the stakes they could seize. Our men who were on foot attacked the tent on all sides, so that there was great confusion around it, and then the horsemen chased [Indians] who escaped."[5]

Castañeda seemed appalled by the killing of all Arenal prisoners. He reported, "Not a man of them remained alive, unless it was some who remained hidden in the village and escaped that night to spread throughout the land that the strangers did not respect the peace that they had made."

After Arenal, Tiwa warriors never again surrendered during the Tiguex War. Although outnumbered and with inferior weapons, Tiwa warriors would fight to the death.

---

[4] R. Flint, *No Settlement, No Conquest*, 148-149. Also, Castañeda, *Journey of Coronado*, 51. Also, "Juan de Contreras, Fifth *de Oficio* Witness" in R. Flint, *Great Cruelties*, 113-114. This burning alive of war prisoners, which might have been common a century earlier in Europe (for example, Joan of Arc in 1431 and the Spanish Inquisition), was considered in Spain "an act of great cruelty" in Day, "Mota Padilla on the Coronado Expedition," 100. Burning of prisoners at Arenal and at Moho was included in war crimes charged against Coronado and Cárdenas.

[5] Castañeda, *Journey of Coronado*, page 51. Expeditionary testimonies reported varying numbers of Tiwas in the tent at the investigation of war crimes charged against Coronado. But it's clear there were scores of Indians killed inside the tent, even if not the hundred reported by Castañeda. Reports of the number of Indians burned alive at the stake also varied from thirty to fifty or more.

* * *

The fall of Ghufoor and Arenal made it clear that all Indian villages were in danger of being attacked. In the days afterward, Xauían persuaded all Tiwas to unite against the expedition's relentless demands for food and clothing. Each pueblo had its own leader in war, so designating Xauían to lead all of them was an extraordinary act of confidence in him. A Spanish historian, Friar Antonio Tello, wrote more than three hundred years later that Tiwas followed "the effort and good leadership of Juan Alemán [Xauían] who always was understood to be the one who advised them."[7]

Castañeda reported that after Arenal it snowed so much that it was impossible to do anything except travel to Tiguex pueblos and advise the Indians to make peace and tell them that they would be pardoned and should consider themselves safe. Castañeda wrote that the Indian response always was the same: "They did not trust those who did not know how to keep good faith after they had once given it, and that the Spaniards should remember that they were keeping [Bigotes] prisoner and that they did not keep their word when they burned those who surrendered [at Arenal]."[8] Overnight, Tiwas abandoned most Tiguex pueblos. Those Puebloans feared that to remain was to invite attack. They fled to snow-covered Sandia Mountain, and perhaps also to the nearby Manzano and Jemez mountains, or to surrounding pueblo villages of the Keres, Tano, Tewa, Towa, Piro, and Tompiro tribes.

Coronado's expedition then attacked some occupied Tiwa pueblos, one by one. Ghufoor and Arenal were only the first two. Coronado ordered attacking of

---

[7] Tello. *Libro Segundo*, 426.

[8] Castañeda, *Journey of Coronado*, 52.

pueblos where, like Ghufoor and Arenal, Tiwas refused to give up without a fight.

Puebloans were secure from attack in the mountains during winter. Conquistador Juan de Zaldivar testified later in regard to the second winter, and presumably also for the first winter of 1540-1541, expeditionaries "did not dare to go to the mountains for fear of their enemies and the deep snow."[9]

* * *

The growing resistance against Europeans presaged the Pueblo Revolt of 1680, when an Indian religious leader named Po'pay (sometimes spelled as Popé or Po'Pay) organized Puebloans to rise up one hundred and thirty years later to drive colonists out of New Mexico. Xauían's Puebloans revolted against Coronado's expedition in 1540-1542. But the courageous opposition of Xauían's forces was overshadowed, and to a degree even forgotten by Puebloans themselves, by the drama of successfully expelling European colonists in 1680 out of what would be New Mexico.[10] Consequently, the Tiguex War is one of the most ignored wars in US history.

Xauían and the Tiwas were a discouraged and isolated people in 1540. Without the advantage of Po'pay's large alliance of all Puebloan villages plus local Apaches, the firepower of the invaders of their country had defeated Tiwa pueblos twice.

---

[9] "Juan de Zaldívar, Twelfth *de Officio* Witness," in R. Flint, *Great Cruelties*, 257. Also, Castañeda de Nájera's Narrative," Flint and Flint, *Documents*, 402.

[10] Many Puebloan students who read Dennis Herrick's historical novel titled *Winter of the Metal People,* which gives the Puebloan point of view to Coronado's expedition, confused that book as an account instead of the Pueblo Revolt, even though those two events were separated by nearly one and a half centuries. Author David Roberts in *The Pueblo Revolt* tried to explain this disconnect by younger Puebloans with their own history.

Pueblos in the Tiguex Province were attacked or so threatened with attack that inhabitants abandoned most. Ghufoor was not attacked a second time because it became Coronado's headquarters called Coofor, and the Tiquex pueblo of Isleta was neutral during the war.

Archaeologists never had the opportunity to excavate pueblos in the 1900s such as Sandia, Puaray, Maigua, or parts of Watche or the first Alameda to see if they were attacked. The locations of Arenal and Moho remain speculative. Archaeologists have not excavated their presumed locations.

* * *

Like the Tiguex Province, the Tiguex War was named after the Tigua (Tiwa) Indians. Expeditionaries, waged war without mercy, killing hundreds of Tiwa warriors in battle. Historian Richard Flint estimated that ten percent of Tiwa population, mostly male warriors, died. Many Tiwas were burned alive at the stake or in their homes. Expeditionaries testified that Coronado ordered several Tiwas to be killed by fierce war dogs similar to a greyhound and known as a *galgo*. There were accounts of expedition members maiming several Tiwa warrior captives by cutting off their hands and noses. Many Tiwas also must have died of starvation or exposure after fleeing to mountain sanctuaries for safety. Spaniards often, but not always, spared women and children in the war so that expedition members could enslave them as war captives.

This book's brevity is the result of Castañeda being the expedition's main chronicler and the Puebloan side never being recorded. Castañeda's forty pages about the war were written more than twenty years after the expedition. He was not present when some events about which he wrote took place, so much is second-hand information told to him by other conquistadors. Later

Spanish historians made brief references to the war, and they are mentioned in this book.

History is silent on why Isleta Pueblo, the largest Tiguex community consisting of several villages at that time, was not drawn into the fighting. Isleta and pueblos outside Tiguex Province did refuse to provide warriors to help Coronado fight the Tiwas. Nevertheless, Xuaían's Tiwas were left to fight on their own.

Because Viceroy Mendoza had ordered Coronado to treat Indians benevolently, many attacks were never reported to the viceroy.[11]

An arquebusier fires a matchlock arquebus musket. The weapon's barrel in Coronado's expedition was heavier and about twice as long. The arquebus (harquebus) was in common use in European, Ottoman Empire, and Asian armies by the 1500s. Notice the tripod stick used to support the heavy iron barrel.

Hundreds of years later, archaeologists would recover from Ghufoor, as well as from Chamisal, Piedras Marcadas and Kuaua pueblos, several fired arquebus musket balls and crossbow points, broken pieces of Spanish armor and weapons, where evidence of combat against villages never had been reported.

---

[11] The viceroy who sent the Coronado expedition, Antonio de Mendoza y Pacheco, died in Peru in 1552, a few years before Castañeda wrote his account. Mendoza was the king's representative in the "New World." The title of viceroy stood for "vice king."

* * *

Eventually, Xauían made sure that Coronado learned that a pueblo on a mesa summit remained in defiance of the expedition.

The most chronicled battle would be fought between the expedition and Xauían's force at this pueblo, referred to in expedition chronicles as "Moho." The pueblo stronghold seemed designed as a fortification that Puebloans used when attacked by enemies. Like Arenal, Moho's original name never was recorded.

—Aerial photo from Google Earth

Three walls still mark the site of Basalt Point, which some researchers believe was the 1541 last-stand Tiwa pueblo that the Spaniards called "Moho." The east edge of a 200-foot cliff can be seen in this aerial view dropping down to the Rio Grande on the far right. The east wall might have been a wooden palisade.

It's known the Keres Indians used this fortified pueblo as a refuge after the Pueblo Revolt 139 years after Coronado's Moho.

Historians Richard Flint and Shirley Cushing Flint have concluded that Moho was a pueblo known now as Basalt Point on the high Santa Ana Mesa overlooking the Rio Grande. Some Spaniards called it Moho, but others called it *Pueblo del Cerco*, which could mean "Besieged Pueblo" or "Pueblo of the Siege" or "Pueblo of the Surrounded Wall."

The fortress location is indicated by its description as being at a height. *Moho* (also spelled mojo) was probably a Castilian word during the sixteenth century referring to rust, the red color of some lichens, a plant found on mountains or high mesas.[12] However, today the word in Spanish refers to mold.

Although not mentioned in the chronicles—possibly because Spaniards would not have known what to make of it—a blood-spattered ogre katsina named Atoshle that originated at Zuni might have appeared on Moho's ramparts. Some Puebloans relied on the fierce-looking Atoshle katsina to warn away enemies.

Coronado or some other conquistador read the *requerimiento* in Spanish three times to Xauían and others lining Moho's walls before starting hostilities.

The requerimiento ended: *"With the help of God, we shall powerfully enter into your country, and shall make war against you in all ways and manners that we can, and shall subject you to the yoke and obedience of the Church and of Their Highnesses. We shall take you and your wives and your children, and shall make slaves of them, and as such shall sell and dispose of them as their Highnesses may command. And we shall take away your goods, and shall do you all the mischief and damage that we can. And we protest that the deaths and losses which shall accrue from this are your fault, and not that of Their Highnesses, or ours, nor of these cavaliers who come with us."*[13]

Spaniards reported that Xauían always defied their threats and demands. In legal proceedings a few years later against Coronado, they characterized Xauían's response as saying the Tiwas "were not familiar with His

---

[12] Cobus, Rubén. *A Dictionary*, 113. Also, "Moho and the Tiguex War," in Richard Flint and Shirley Cushing Flint, eds., *The Latest Word*, 361.

[13] The word "requerimiento" in Spanish is used more like the English word of "ultimatum." For a full text of the *requerimiento*, which Spaniards used for decades to assert hegemony over Indians and require their conversion to Catholicism, go to http://en.wikipedia.org/wiki/Requerimiento.

Majesty, and did not want to serve him" or any other Christian.[14]

Moho's defenders knew how Cárdenas had slaughtered everyone at Arenal. Xauían crafted a plan for revenge. Castañeda described what happened when Xauían invited Cárdenas to a negotiation.

Only Spanish chronicles biased against Indians exist to tell of a dramatic encounter at Moho between Cárdenas for the expedition and Xauían for the Tiwas.

Castañeda wrote: "Cárdenas started out with about thirty companions and went to [Moho] to talk with Juan Alemán. (Castañeda always referred to Xauían as Juan Alemán.) Although [the Tiwas] were hostile, they ... said that if he [Cárdenas] wished to talk with them he must dismount from his horse and they would come out and talk with him about a peace, and that if he would send away the horsemen and make his men keep away, Juan Alemán [Xauían] and another captain would come out of the village and meet him. Everything was done as they required, and then when they approached they said that they had no arms and that he must take his off. [Cárdenas] did this in order to give them confidence."

Castañeda continued: "Juan Alemán [Xauían] approached and embraced [Cárdenas] vigorously, while the other two who had come with him drew two mallets which they had hidden behind their backs and gave [Cárdenas] two such blows over his helmet that they almost knocked him senseless. Two of the soldiers on horseback ... rode up so quickly ... and hurriedly carried off their captain, without being able to harm the enemy ... while many of our men were dangerously

---

14 "Defense Offered by Vázquez de Coronado." R. Flint, *Great Cruelties*, 354.

wounded" by a shower of arrows from Moho."[15]

Castañeda reported, "The Indians paid no attention to the demands made on them except by shooting arrows from the upper stories with loud yells, and would not hear of peace." The horsemen then backed off a distance but others remained to stop anyone from coming out of Moho.

Missing from Castañeda's one-sided account makes Xauían and companions with their clubs look treacherous. It doesn't point out that Cárdenas also went to the meeting armed with a concealed dagger.

Cárdenas eventually left with part of the force to another village, which one conquistador named *Pueblo de la Cruz* about half a league distant (about one and half miles). Castañeda reported Tiwas also had gathered in rebellion at that second pueblo. Castañeda doesn't specify "distant" from where—whether distant from Moho or from Coronado's headquarters at Ghufoor/Coofor, where Castañeda was stationed.

When Cárdenas returned to Moho, Castañeda reported that Cárdenas then used a common Spanish cavalry battle tactic. "When a large number of those in the village came out ... our men rode off slowly, pretending to flee, so that they drew the enemy on to the plain, and then turned on them and [killed] several." Cárdenas returned to Ghufoor/Coofor to report to Coronado that Moho would not come to what Spaniards considered "obedience."

A few days later Coronado led expeditionaries to Moho with scaling ladders, mustering hundreds of Europeans and Mexican Indian warriors. Coronado's force found a way for his horses to ascend to the top of the mesa onto a grassy plain in front of Moho. The

---

[15] Castañeda, *Journey of Coronado*, 53.

Tiwa bastion was perched at the mesa's east end at the edge of a steep cliff that dropped about two hundred feet to the Rio Grande.

Coronado wanted to mount an overwhelming attack with cavalry and men-at-arms on foot so that victory would be swift. That was so the expedition could avoid a long time atop the wind-swept mesa during a brutal winter.

However, instead of dried mud adobe, like the river valley's pueblos, Moho was built of basalt blocks from an old lava flow that was impervious to battering rams or fire. A palisade of logs might have blocked the cliff side.

It shocked Coronado to see the first attack fail, useless as a wave crashing against a cliff. Moho had firing loopholes, desert prairie in front of it that could be riddled with arrows, and defensive measures that exposed attackers who reached the roof to a crossfire of arrows and to rocks thrown down from higher towers. Spanish historian Matías de la Mota Padilla later described Moho's formidable defensive features from documents now lost.[16]

Three or four Spaniards and unnumbered Mexican Indian warriors were killed in the first assault. Mexican Indian warriors suffered the most casualties because they spearheaded Tiguex War attacks against pueblos, diminishing European casualties. Castañeda rarely reported Mexican Indian allies' assistance or casualties, but Coronado testified at his 1544 investigation, saying there were "fewer than thirty" deaths of Mexican Indian

---

[16] Day, "Mota Padilla on the Coronado Expedition," 100. The historian commonly designated himself as Mota Padilla, but his full Spanish name was Matías Ángel de la Mota López Padilla.

allies during the expedition.[17] Scores of Mexican Indian allies and Spaniards also were wounded at Moho before Coronado called back the first attack. Castañeda reported that some wounded men died.

That assault and others against Moho resulted in the greatest pitched battles between Europeans and Indian warriors in American Southwest history, as well as its longest military siege. Approximate casualty figures were reported during testimony against Coronado in the investigation of him in 1544–46 at Mexico City. Castañeda gave no specific casualty figures for Mexican Indian allies or Spaniards. However, expeditionary members later reported "seven" or "twelve to fifteen" Spaniards were killed in the initial assault and during the siege. The numbers of wounded Spaniards varied from "more than sixty" to "seventy or eighty." No specific estimates were given for Mexican Indian allies killed in the first attack.

Castañeda reported, "One day when there was a hard fight, they killed Francisco de Ovando, a captain who had been [*maestre de campo*] all the time that García López de Cárdenas was away … and also Francisco Pobares, a fine gentleman." Castañeda revealed, "Our men were unable to prevent them from carrying Francisco de Ovando inside the village."

When Ovando's body was recovered later, preserved by the cold, the only wounds inflicted were those that killed him and a finger cut off to take a ring. As for Pobares, his death occurred when he tried to plug a loophole in one wall with handfuls of mud and an arrow fired through the mud struck him in the eye, killing him instantly.

---

[17] R. Fint, *Great Cruelties*, 526. It's impossible to know if that was an accurate estimation.

The Spaniards sent repeated attacks against the Moho refuge into early January 1541. They were unable to breach it because of its construction with basalt rock.

A Spanish historian later wrote, "They ... built some engines with timbers which they called swings, like the old rams with which they battered fortresses in times before gunpowder ... but they did no good. Then, lacking artillery, they attempted to make some wooden tubes tightly bound on the order of rockets, but these did not serve either."[18]

Unable to overrun Moho, the expedition settled in with a siege. That siege, probably with more attacks, lasted for about eighty days.

The siege force must have spent great effort obtaining firewood to survive winter atop the mesa, pulling beams and other wood from abandoned pueblos in the desert along the Rio Grande. At some point, Coronado returned to the relative warmth and comfort of Coofor for an unspecified time before returning to Moho.

Castañeda reported that several weeks into the siege the Moho defenders "asked to speak to us, and said that, since they knew we would not harm the women and children, they wished to surrender [them], because they were using up their water."

Castañeda wrote about the restraint of Indians and the courage of one horseman, Lope de Urrea.

After the women and children "who did not want to leave" were sent to Urrea, Castañeda wrote that [the

---

[18] Day. "Mota Padilla on the Coronado Expedition," 101–102. These comments imply that the expedition's pedrero stone-throwing cannons were not fired at Moho. Earlier comments by Castañeda implies they were fired at Hawikku, and they might have been used against Ghufoor and Arenal. However, there is no chronicle record to indicate they were fired against those latter two pueblos.

defenders told Urrea] "to go away, as they did not wish to trust themselves to people who had no regard for friendship or their own word which they had pledged. As [Urrea] seemed unwilling to go away, one of [the Tiwas] put an arrow in his bow ... and threatened to shoot him ... unless he went off. [Other horsemen farther back] warned him to put on his helmet, but he was unwilling to do so, saying that they would not hurt him as long as he stayed there. When the Indian saw that [Urrea] did not want to go away, he shot and planted his arrow between the forefeet of the horse, and then put another arrow in his bow and repeated that if he did not go away he would really shoot him. [Urrea] put on his helmet and slowly rode back to where the horsemen were, without receiving any harm."[19]

Castañeda added, "It was impossible to persuade them to make peace, as they said that the Spaniards would not keep an agreement made with them."

Urrea took the hundred or so women and children back to expedition members, who distributed them as forced labor/slaves to officers and several conquistadors.

During the siege, Castañeda reported, "A Spaniard named Cervantes, who had charge of [Turk] during the siege, solemnly swore that he had seen the Turk talking with the devil in a pitcher of water." Several expedition members believed the story.[20]

Castañeda rationalized the ability of Tiwas to withstand such a long siege by claiming Moho defenders "dug a very deep well inside the village, but were not

---

[19] Castañeda, *Journey of Coronado*, 55–56.

[20] Ibid., 62–63. This incident was believed by many on the expedition, revealing that at least some expeditionaries were as superstitious as they considered the Puebloans to be.

able to get water, and while they were making it, it fell in and killed 30 persons."[21] Such a well might be a Spanish myth, however, because it defies common sense that conquistadors would undertake the arduous and dangerous task of digging into a collapsed well just to count Indian bodies. Castañeda's so-called "well" was perhaps a roofless room that collected years of snow and rainfall, because no trace of a well can be seen at the Basalt Point site thought now to have been Moho.

Regardless, thirst, rather than attacks, forced Tiwas to abandon their stronghold after nearly three months.

Fifteen days after the women and children were given up, Xauían organized a night escape attempt in middle or late March 1541.[22] The escape probably was scheduled during the darkness of a clouded-over night or perhaps during the New Moon. Tiwas climbed down the mesa cliff and then ran to the nearby river. The men formed a line around women as they ran from Moho. Spaniards spotted them in the darkness and raised an alarm. The Tiwas did kill one Spaniard and one horse and wounded others, although most Tiwa warriors went down fighting.

Castañeda's account of cavalry response to the escape attempt was that Tiwa occupants of Moho "were

---

[21] Ibid., 54–55. Also, Day, "Mota Padilla on the Coronado Expedition," 102, reported that Spaniards discovered a well had been dug in Moho's plaza, but Mota Padilla made no mention of it having caved in. No evidence of a well cavity can be seen on aerial photographs of locations proposed as Moho's site.

[22] Castañeda claimed the Moho siege lasted forty-five days, but others report it lasted for eighty days. The siege began in early January, so if it ended in mid to late March the eighty-day figure would be more accurate. Very likely, the escape occurred on or about March 28, 1541, in the present-day Gregorian calendar. That New Moon would have been on or about March 18 in the Julian calendar used at the time of the expedition. Castañeda reported, "This siege ended the last of March."

driven back with great slaughter until they came to the river, where the water flowed swiftly and very cold ... [The Indians] threw themselves into this, and as the men had come quickly from the whole camp to assist the cavalry, there were few who escaped being killed or wounded."[23]

Castañeda wrote that stopping the escape attempt ended the siege. However, a few Tiwas remained in one part of Moho. They were killed or captured a few days later when expeditionaries stormed Moho's nearly abandoned stronghold.

Xauían was killed in the escape's battle. Xauían's death is assumed, because Castañeda frequently mentioned him until Moho but never afterward.[24]

A few men and women were found in the morning on the opposite bank helpless from wounds or cold. Expeditionary Rodrigo Ximón testified three years later that the Europeans "lanced, stabbed, and set dogs on [those incapacitated Indians]."[25] Historian Richard Flint noted how Ximón apparently "was certain those actions were both reasonable and legal."[26] More candid about his attitude than other expeditionaries who testified, Ximón's comments revealed the feeling of at least some expeditionaries that Indians were not humans and they deserved a cruel death if they resisted the expedition.

After several testified to the killing or maiming of

---

[23] Castañeda, *Journey of Coronado*, 57.

[24] Most historians don't write about Xauían's leadership during the Tiguex War. When he is mentioned, they often use the nickname of "Juan Alemán" that the Spaniards gave him in the chronicles, instead of his actual Tiwa name of Xauían. Coronado's field master gave Xauían's Tiwa name in a Spanish jail cell deposition five years later in 1546.

[25] "Rodrigo Xímón, Sixth *de Oficio* Witness," R. Flint, *Great Cruelties*, 132.

[26] Ibid.,127.

Moho escapees, Pedro de Ledesma testified about the lancing of scores of Zunis at Cíbola/Hawikku, burning Indians at the stake at Arenal, and siccing war dogs on Bigotes to bite him. But on page 241 of *Great Cruelties*, Ledesma finished by insisting, "He did not see [anyone on the expedition] commit any outrages." Flint noted that Ledesma felt that "none of the Spaniards ... had anything to regret ... with regard to treatment of the Indians."

Fifteen expedition members testified at the war crimes investigation against Coronado in Mexico City, with some of those key testimonies described in the following paragraphs.

The charges included wanton killing of the last Moho defenders by burning them inside their houses, killing attempted escapees with dogs, and stabbings. They also admitted tortuous maiming by cutting off the hands and noses of about ten male prisoners of war.

Expeditionary Domingo Martín swore in 1544, "The pueblo laid siege to [Moho] ... was burned, a great many Indians inside their houses because [the conquistadors] could not subdue them without setting fire to the pueblo. And the Indians were doing significant damage [to expeditionaries] from their houses." But concerning Tiwas captured alive, [Martín] did not see that any were burned, "except a few as punishment. And to put fear in the rest, [expedition members] cut off their hands."[27]

A historian noted, "Martín consistently maintained that Vásquez de Coronado had behaved properly ... in

27 "Domingo Martín, Fourth *de Oficio* Witness," R. Flint, *Great Cruelties*, 96.

line with the rest of the witnesses" who were summoned for Coronado's defense.[28]

Expedition horseman Rodrigo de Frías testified, "Some who were captured during the siege were burned and set upon by dogs, and also [some Indian men] had their hands cut off."[29]

Teenager and standard bearer Alonso Álvarez testified that at Moho "He knows and saw that ... two or three Indians were set upon by dogs and another nine or ten had their hands and noses cut off. He believes that the unleashing of dogs was carried out under [Coronado's] order. ... Francisco Vázquez ordered [expeditionaries to cut off Indian hands and noses]. He ordered each [of the crippled Indians then released] ... so that [other Tiwas] might see what punishment" had been inflicted for rebelling.[30]

Coronado testified that he knew nothing of those events. He declared in a sworn statement that he gave the Indians "thoroughly benevolent treatment."

In the 1700s, Spanish historian Matías de la Mota Padilla criticized Coronado, writing, "And thus one night the besieged went forth in flight, leaving our people fooled and with no gain. ... and Indians went out valorously."[31]

Some who managed to escape and those who were maimed told other Tiwas hiding in the mountains and at

---

[28] Ibid., 90.

[29] "Alonso Álvarez, Fourteenth *de Oficio* Witness," in R. Flint, *Great Cruelties*, 318-319. Much of Spanish strategy was intended to terrorize Indians. See "The Nominal Target of the Investigation, Francisco Vázquez de Coronado," in R. Flint, *Great Cruelties*, 291, where Coronado denied his fellow expeditionaries' testimonies that Indians who fled Moho were killed or maimed.

[30] Day. "Mota Padilla on the Coronado Expedition," 102.

[31] Flint and Flint, *The Latest Word*, 354.

non-attacked villages what happened.

Xauían had achieved strategic victory with his sacrifice. He had tied down the expedition all winter, preventing Coronado from attacking Tiwas during their most vulnerable time in the mountains.

Eyewitness accounts had reported Ghufoor/Coofor and Moho were about four leagues apart. A Spanish league was a distance counted by footsteps, so its use in Spanish chronicles is unreliable. It is four and a half leagues, about eleven miles, in a straight-line distance northward from Ghufoor/Coofor to Basalt Point.

Spaniards reported Moho was a "very strong pueblo" that was difficult to attack because it was *un alto* —that is, on a height. Such a description implies that Moho might have been unlike any other regular valley pueblo. Instead, it might have been a secluded stronghold built for a final defense against invaders.

Pueblos fitting that description include Basalt Point and some other mesa pedestals on or by the Santa Ana Mesa that sit atop steeply sided promontories. Basalt Point is atop high Santa Ana Mesa north of today's San Felipe Pueblo, which did not exist in Coronado's time.

Coronado researcher Carroll Riley suggested in 1995 that one of the ruins on or around Santa Ana Mesa north of the Jemez River might have been Moho, although he was not certain which ruin.

Richard Flint and Shirley Cushing Flint, key researchers of the Coronado expedition, are convinced that Moho was located at Basalt Point on the steep edge atop Santa Ana Mesa. Riley and the Flints agreed that Ghufoor/Coofor, later to be called Santiago Pueblo, could not have been Moho despite some early historians thinking so.

"Documentary evidence that Santiago's perch on its

50-foot bluff [on its east side] would not have qualified as '*un alto*' is provided by the expeditionaries' descriptions of Acoma [atop its 365-foot mesa] as the strongest place in the world," Richard Flint wrote. He concluded, "[Moho's] situation on an elevation with difficult access contributed significantly to the inability of the expeditionaries to subdue it by sheer force."[32]

Meanwhile, back at Moho, expeditionaries plundered the fortification, burning warriors in their houses and capturing the surviving women and children as prisoners to serve as "servants" to expedition members.

* * *

A few conquistadors claimed that expeditionaries attacked at least one other additional besieged pueblo, implying rightly or wrongly that it might have been near Moho and assaulted at the same time in early 1541. But only Frías gave a name for a second besieged pueblo during testimony at the investigation of Coronado.

Castañeda had reported that another besieged pueblo was overrun, but he doesn't give a name. After Moho, Castañeda reported two captains, Diego de Guevara and Juan de Zaldivar, captured a second besieged village. Castañeda wrote, "Having started out very early one morning to make an ambuscade in which to catch some warriors who used to come out every morning to try to frighten our camp, the spies, who had been placed where they could see when [Puebloans] were coming, saw the people come out and proceed toward the country. The soldiers left the ambuscade and went to the village and saw the people fleeing. They pursued and killed large numbers of them."

Because his account was written more than two

---

[32] Ibid., 354.

decades after the expedition, it's possible that what Castañeda called an additional pueblo was actually Arenal, or that he confused details for that pueblo with details about attacks against Ghufoor or another pueblo.

Frías was a cavalryman like Castañeda. In his 1544 testimony, Frías gave a name to a second besieged village as *Pueblo de la Cruz*, which means "Village of the Cross" in English. Frías never spoke of a location. Adding to confusion, he gave different names than others did for pueblos such as Ghufoor/Coofor, Arenal, and Moho. And although he referred to Pueblo de la Cruz as an additional besieged pueblo, he also testified that only three pueblos were assaulted during the war, although archaeologists four centuries later found evidence that at least four or five pueblos were attacked in addition to the pre-war assault on Ghufoor/Coofor.

Castañeda wrote that his second besieged pueblo was overcome in March 1541. It's usually assumed he meant March 1542 because he often was a year off in his dates. If so, perhaps he was referring to an attack against Piedras Marcadas Pueblo in what is now northeast Albuquerque. That attack also never was reported in the chronicles, and it might have occurred shortly before Coronado retreated to Mexico.

"Here [whether at Kuaua, Piedras Marcadas, or elsewhere] the Indians also attempted to escape at night," wrote W.W.H. Davis in his 1869 history. Davis repeated Castañeda's version, writing, "But [in the attempted escape] they were discovered by the Spaniards who laid in ambush, who sallied out and attacked them. A great number were killed and the rest put to flight ... about one hundred women and children were made prisoners."[33]

---

[33] Davis. *The Spanish Conquest,* 198.

Details remain confusing because of Castañeda's unclear style of writing and Davis's vague recap of Castañeda's account. A second besieged pueblo if it existed remains a mystery and details remain unclear.[34] What Tiwa village was Pueblo de la Cruz? At a distance of about five centuries and without adequate documentation, it can't be known for certain.

Archaeologist Clay Mathers believes it's possible that Pueblo de la Cruz was Kuaua Pueblo at today's Coronado Historic Site near Bernalillo, New Mexico. Mathers discovered fired arquebus musket balls and crossbow points and other signs of 1500s combat, up to Kuaua's walls. He also found an obsidian arrowhead sharpened by knapping its edges that is believed to be of Mexican origin.

Kuaua never had been suspected before of being one of the pueblos attacked by the expedition.

In the original excavation and partial restoration of Kuaua Pueblo in the 1930s, excavating was done only on and inside the pueblo's foundations. But Mathers's further excavations in 2017–2019 took place outside Kuaua's walls. Regardless of whether Mathers is correct that Pueblo de la Cruz was Kuaua, his archaeological research proves that an unreported attack occurred at Kuaua Pueblo.

Also, Albuquerque archaeologist Matt Schmader used metal detectors in 2007 and found fired crossbow points, arquebus balls, and other evidence to determine that Coronado's force had attacked Piedras Marcadas Pueblo in northwest Albuquerque. The attack breached

---

[34] Spanish references to a second stronghold are contradictory. Adding to confusion, Castañeda also used the term of Tiguex for different villages inside the province, such as Moho, so it's sometimes difficult to tell if he is writing about a village or the entire province.

the north wall. No Spanish chronicle records such an attack by Spaniards and their Mexican Indian allies.[35]

The expedition also conquered at least one other pueblo, Chamisal, where evidence of combat has been found, and another village that has not yet been confirmed. Arenal was a fifth attacked pueblo. Ghufoor was attacked, although that attack is not counted as one of the Tiguex War battles.

Expeditionary members in their testimonies never mentioned attacks against more than Ghufoor/Coofor, Arenal, Moho, and possibly Pueblo de la Cruz.

* * *

It's likely that Europeans and Indians on both sides spoke degrees of fluency in Nahuatl, the language of the Aztecs, many of whom were on the expedition, and/or Piman dialects. Like English today, Piman and Nahuatl were universal trade languages throughout at least northern Mexico and the present southwestern US. Castañeda believed that even the Pawnee Turk knew some Nahuatl.

Many Mexican Indians also were fluent in Spanish or knew key Spanish words. Puebloans often knew neighboring pueblos' languages. Even when spoken languages were not possible, Castañeda wrote, "They are able to make themselves very well understood by means of (hand) signs." On the Great Plains, expeditionary Juan Jaramillo said it was easy to understand Apaches who used the universal Indian hand signs.[36]

Forced labor and chattel slavery were key

---

[35] Mathers. "The grammar and syntax."

[36] "Narrative of Jaramillo" reprinted in Castañeda, *Journey of Coronado*, 232. Castañeda's observation is on page 112. For an analysis of communication, see R. Flint, *No Settlement, No Conquest*, 81-85.

trademarks of Spanish domination. Both are often interchangeable terms.

Differences are that forced labor was work performed involuntarily. But unlike slavery, "forced labor" did not involve ownership of a person by another. Any technical distinction between the two was not apparent to Indians required to work at Spanish plantations, mines, and households, or for expeditions.

Slavery and forced labor were not unique to Europeans in the Americas. Even the Indians had varying versions of forced labor and even slavery. Two examples are Aztecs and Mayans, who sometimes sold even forced laborers for ritual sacrifice. Because Indian commoners had no money, and often few goods, Indian "tribute" often was in forced labor.[37]

Viceroy Mendoza had specifically ordered Coronado to not enslave Indians. Coronado freed all Puebloans who had been forced laborers and slaves taken in the Tiguex War before returning to Mexico. He wanted to avoid the viceroy discovering Coronado's men had used prisoners as forced labor "servants."

Odds fighting Europeans were formidable for Indians facing superior numbers and technology. The Tiguex War marked the beginning of about four hundred years of wars against Indians for possession of what is now the United States.

The wars were conflicts of population and superior technology on the non-Indian side—first by the Europeans and then the Americans. The millions of Euro-Americans could replace combatants lost in battle with recruits, but it could take Indians a generation to replace an experienced warrior.

---

[37] See Chapter 19, "Inhumane Bondage and Historical Context" in Herrick, *Esteban: The African Slave*, 199-207.

4 **AFTERMATH**

Xauían's presumed death ended only the main phase of the Tiguex War.

After the fall of Moho, Coronado sent men to the Rio Grande Valley's Keres, Tano, Tewa, Towa, Piro, and Tompiro pueblos that had not been attacked during the war to assure them that—despite his warfare against Tiwa pueblos—Coronado was a friend. Puebloans remained wary. According to Castañeda, the twelve Tiwa villages of Tiguex Province were not repopulated during this time "in spite of every promise of security that could possibly be given to them."

The Tiwas who abandoned their pueblos and escaped to their mountain sanctuary and neighboring pueblos would participate in a pivotal role in guerrilla warfare during the next winter of 1541–42.

After conquering Moho, Coronado decided to travel across the Great Plains to Quivira to find Turk's rumored gold.[1] The Rio Grande had been frozen for four months, so people, horses, and the expedition's sheep crossed the river ice.

A few days later, expedition members had to build a

---

[1] Castañeda, *Journey of Coronado*, 62.

bridge over the spring-melt flooded Pecos River.[2] During that spring and summer of 1541, Coronado led the expedition into present-day Texas.

The Pawnee Turk, who'd told Coronado that gold could be found on the other side of the Great Plains, had inflamed the expedition's gold fever. Excited by Turk's stories, Coronado took everyone, including captive Tiwa women and children, into western Texas with Turk as guide.

On the Great Plains, Coronado encountered apparent Apache bands that Spaniards called as Querechos and Teyas. They showed no fear of the expedition's horse-bound conquistadors. Castañeda reported, "Although they conversed by means of signs, they made themselves understood so well that there was no need of an interpreter."[3]

The expedition and captives endured a devastating hailstorm in what is Blanco Canyon about thirty-five miles northeast of modern Lubbock, Texas. Coronado is reported to have moved everyone to Palo Duro Canyon then, near present Amarillo, Texas.

Some historians have thought that Turk conspired with some Puebloans to lead Coronado away from pueblo lands. An early exhibit at the modern-day Indian Pueblo Cultural Center in Albuquerque read, "We [Puebloans] were able to find a man [Turk] to steer [Coronado] to Kansas to search for gold and riches, but they soon realized that these could not be found, so

---

[2] Ibid, 2. Other bridges probably were built over rivers during the expedition's travels, but this is the only one reported by Castañeda. See also, Flint and Flint, "A remarkable memory of a bridge built by the Coronado Expedition."

[3] Castañeda, *Journey of Coronado*, 65.

they killed our friend."[4]

Coronado decided that Turk was leading the advance force too far to the east and southward. So he replaced Turk with Teya Indian guides who led them northward to Quivira. In Kansas, he had Turk garroted for leading the Spaniards many miles in misdirection. Historians influenced by Spanish chronicles continue to depict Turk as a liar who deserved to be strangled.

But Turk didn't owe any cooperation to his enemies, some of whom had been urging for some time that he be executed.

Expeditionary Gaspar de Saldaña recognized Turk's humanity at the 1544–46 investigation of war crime charges against Coronado, testifying in a *de parte* statement: "[Turk] had wanted to lead them lost by that route so that they would not go to his land to subjugate his parents, relatives, and forebears. [That was] because it was a worthier thing for him to die, so that his relatives would not be subjects of the Christians."[5]

Coronado is believed to have traveled as far as present-day Great Bend, Kansas. He found massive herds of buffalo and straw-thatched huts, but no gold in Quivira. The expedition conducted twenty-five days of reconnaissance all around. Like the Puebloans, however, the Quivirans lived at the subsistence level and were not populous enough for forced-labor encomiendas. Coronado found nothing that could be considered European-style riches. Discouraged, Coronado and his force left Quivira by a different, shorter route across the Great Plains in the late summer led by Quiviran guides.

New *maestre de campo* Tristán de Luna y Arellano led

---

4 A 1990s exhibit seen by the author at the Indian Pueblo Cultural Center at Albuquerque, N.M

5 "Further Defense" in R. Flint, *Great Cruelties,* 445.

the expeditionaries and captives who Coronado had left behind at Palo Duro Canyon, finding their route back to Tiguex Province. Arellano had taken over as second-in-command when Cárdenas broke his shoulder in a fall from his horse.

Tiwas had begun to rebuild their villages during Coronado's absence. But with news that Coronado was returning, they again abandoned their villages and vanished into their mountain sanctuaries and in other tribes' villages.

* * *

Questions remain about some statements in Castañeda's account that are accepted as eyewitness history. In addition to reporting the wrong year on many dates, Castañeda also had other errors in his account. Although presenting his account as if an eyewitness, Castañeda was not where some events took place. He relied on what other conquistadors reported to him. More than twenty years later when he wrote his account, did he misremember some details of what he'd been told? Much confusion has resulted, including the location of any second besieged pueblo during the Tiguex War.

It's surprising that Castañeda reported Coronado entrusted the care of four bronze *pedrero* cannons for safekeeping to Zia, a Keres pueblo. Zia Pueblo still exists at its original location, about fourteen miles northwest of Kuaua. Castañeda referred to the pedreros as "cannons ... in poor condition."[6] Pedrero cannons were smoothbore, fired stone balls, and were light enough to transport on the backs of mules. No record exists of pedrero cannons being used against Moho,

---

[6] Castañeda referred to "artillery" in the battle at Hawikku, which was apparently pedrero cannons fired there, *"Relación del Suceso"* reprinted in Castañeda, *Journey of Coronado*, 199.

61

although they might have been fired there. If so, their stone balls would have been ineffective against Moho's basalt-block walls. The cannons were useless without gunpowder, of course, which Coronado did not send to Zia.

At least one battle occurred after the Tiguex War had technically ended.[7] Awaiting Coronado's return from across the Great Plains, Arellano camped much of the expedition with its Mexican Indian allies in the late summer of 1541 near the large Towa pueblo of Pecos on the western edge of the Great Plains. Perhaps fearing the expedition was about to attack their pueblo as it had the Tiguex pueblos, warriors streamed out of Pecos Pueblo to challenge the conquistadors and their allies.

Castañeda reported the battle lasted four days with two Pecos leaders killed along with several warriors. As usual, expedition casualties were not reported. Arellano eventually ordered several volleys from arquebus muskets and crossbows fired into the village, and the combat stopped.

Arellano resumed waiting to greet Coronado upon the captain general's return from the chimerical quest for gold at Quivira. It was a downcast Coronado who arrived outside of Pecos. Castañeda reported that the only metal found was a Quiviran chief's copper medallion. Copper was traded from what is now the upper peninsula of Michigan throughout many tribes east of the Mississippi River.

The medallion has led some historians to wonder if Turk's reported gold armbands were actually made of

---

[7] R. Flint, *No Settlement, No Conquest*, 183. Also, Castañeda, *Journey of Coronado*, 81.

copper.[8] Spaniards repeatedly also were confused by sixteenth-century Indians who often spoke of their oral tradition's lore of the past as if it was contemporary with the present—telling the Spaniards of great Indian cities that no longer existed as if they were still there. Spaniards thought Indians were lying, but Indians might have used a different sense of time than Europeans. Perhaps in talking about Quivira, Turk actually might have been referring to the prosperous and populous mound builders culture farther east in Illinois at Cahokia, a thriving Indian city of the Mississippian Culture. However, Cahokia ceased existence about two hundred years before Coronado's expedition.

Several expeditionaries were disappointed that no gold was found at Quivira. Coronado explained that he "had not dared to enter [farther] into the [Quivira] country on account of its being thickly settled and his force not very strong." It took Coronado's advance force forty days to return empty-handed from Kansas to Pecos Pueblo, where Arellano waited.

Coronado then went on to Tiguex Province in July or August and discovered the Tiwas had been alerted to his return. He found a province of ghost towns with harvested and burned crop fields, as well as Tiwa warriors from the mountains waging hit-and-run

---

[8] Ibid, 163-164. Richard Flint and at least one other historian theorize that the armbands were made of copper, not gold. Flint also theorized that Turk was repeating oral tradition to Alvarado and Coronado about ancient Cahokia.

guerrilla raids against the expedition.[9] With no Tiwa pueblos left to mass its forces against, expeditionaries were unable to effectively respond. And they did not go into the mountains because of deep snow, as an expeditionary had testified at Coronado's investigation.[10]

Castañeda reported that non-Tiguex pueblos that had not been attacked by Coronado in the war began refusing to provide food and supplies to the expedition during the second winter. Unlike the first winter when residents of those pueblos were intimidated into giving necessary food and supplies to Coronado's force, now the continuing Tiwa resistance in guerrilla warfare encouraged them to refuse supplies in the second winter. That resulted in the dire circumstances of the expedition's dwindling resources.[11]

As one researcher noted, Coronado's return from the Great Plains led to expedition members complaining that uncooperative Puebloans stayed behind their pueblos' walls, making expedition threats embarrassing because the expedition no longer had military power needed to enforce demands. Castañeda reported, "The soldiers were almost naked and poorly clothed, full of

---

[9] Spanish chronicles are silent about any guerrilla warfare during the second autumn and winter. But expeditionary testimonies in the investigation of Coronado for war crimes provided evidence of continuing warfare. So does the *Royal Audiencia* charges, stating: "Though they [Tiwas] had been at peace, they returned to war and are so to this day … the Indians killed many Spaniards and everyone was on the verge of being lost." R. Flint, *No Settlement, No Conquest*, 185. Also, "The fiscal's Accusations Against Vázquez de Coronado," in R. Flint. *Great Cruelties*, 330-331.

[10] "Juan de Zaldívar, Twelfth *de Officio* Witness," R. Flint. *Great Cruelties*, 257.

[11] Castañeda, *Journey of Coronado*, 118. Also, R. Flint, *No Settlement, No Conquest*, 186. The expedition had returned with buffalo meat from their Great Plains trek, but that meat eventually was exhausted.

lice, which they were unable to get rid of or avoid."[12] Hunger stalked the expeditionaries after buffalo meat from their Great Plains trek and food from the Tiwa fields was eaten up. The poor conditions resulted in horses dying and men becoming sick. There also might have been a disease outbreak.

Castañeda reported on declining morale with a rare mention of expedition failings. He said expedition members began to grumble that officers were showing favoritism to friends, many expeditionaries were hungry and sick, and complaints emphasized the plague of lice. He wrote, "There began to be some angry murmuring on account of this ... they began to say that there was nothing in the country of Quivira which was worth returning for."[13]

At some point Coronado became incapacitated by a fall from his horse in a race with an officer along the west bank of the Rio Grande near the commandeered pueblo of Ghufoor/Coofor. He remained secluded with a head injury inside his quarters at the commandeered pueblo.

Castañeda wrote, "It was while [Coronado] was in this condition that he recollected what a scientific [astrology] friend of his in Salamanca had told him, that he would become a powerful lord in distant lands, and that he would have a fall from which he would never be able to recover. This expectation of death made him desire to return and die where he had a wife and children."[14]

In early April 1542, his men disheartened, and with

---

12 Ibid., 118.

13 Ibid., 119.

14 Ibid., 120. At that time, astrology was considered scientific, at least in Spain.

both men and horses suffering from reduced rations and dying from disease or other hardships, Coronado's expedition left Coofor on the long and perilous trip to Mexico City.

It was an ignominious retreat from pueblo lands, which had started with such bravado and military victories in the expedition's year and about nine months since the battle at Hawikku. In the retreat back toward Zuni country, the trail was littered with the bodies of dead, undernourished, and possibly diseased horses. Castañeda reported, "More than thirty [horses] died during the ten days which it took to reach Cíbola [Zuni], and there was not a day in which two or three or more did not die."[15]

Many Mexican Indian allies deserted during the retreat. The Chamuscado-Rodriguez expedition forty years later found several Mexican Indians who could speak half-forgotten Spanish and lived in pueblos from Zuni in the west and across three hundred miles east to Pecos Pueblo.

On the return, expedition members had to fight hostile Mexican Caxcan tribes rebelling in the Mixtón War. Castañeda reported that Caxcanes used poison-tipped arrows, killing and wounding several expedition members. An alligator killed one expeditionary at a river crossing.

Pueblo Indians did not harass with even sniper attacks against the expedition on its retreat. Tiwas probably no longer had enough warriors after the Tiguex War. But the biggest reason probably was the same as almost a century and a half later following the Pueblo Revolt of 1680. At that time, Puebloans watched but did not pursue Spanish soldiers and colonists

---

15 Ibid., 127–128.

retreating from Santa Fe to El Paso, Texas. The biggest reason both times was that Puebloans probably were overjoyed to see the invaders leave.

The viceroy in Mexico City declared expeditions unauthorized to pueblo country for half a century after Coronado. There were some limited and illegal expeditions, but Spaniards would not return for permanent settlement until 1598, fifty-six years after Coronado.

Thanks to Xauían's leadership in the Tiguex War, which inspired guerrilla warfare through the second winter, the largest Spanish invasion of native land north of Mexico failed.

Two events unrelated to the Tiguex War occurred in the summer interlude between the expedition's combat of the first winter of 1540–1541 and the Tiwas' guerrilla warfare of the second winter of 1541–1542.

The first incident happened as Coronado and his expedition traveled across the Great Plains on their way to Quivira. The second occurred on the way back.

After twenty days of travel to what is believed to be now west Texas, the Spanish officer Juan Jaramillo reported the first incident. He wrote that the expedition encountered an "old blind [Indian] man." The elderly Indian told Jaramillo by hand signs that he "had seen four others like us many days ago." Jaramillo wrote in his account that he "understood [the elderly Indian] and presumed it was Dorantes and Cabeza de Vaca" with their traveling companions.[16] If Jaramillo was correct, what the old man meant by "many days" was actually twelve years earlier and more than two hundred miles

---

[16] "Translation of the Narrative of Jaramillo," reprinted in Castañeda, *Journey of Coronado*, 232. Also, in *Journey of Coronado*, 68-69. Also, see Herrick, *Esteban: The African Slave*, 86-141.

south in Mexico. The Indians' seasonal and nomadic travels followed the buffalo herds. Jaramillo decided that the elderly Indian had witnessed Spaniards Andrés Dorantes, Álvar Cabeza de Vaca, and Alonso del Castillo Maldonado plus the African slave Esteban. Those four men were walking westward as healers across Mexico through Indian villages on their epic escape as survivors of the failed 1520s Narváez expedition to Florida. Castañeda saw an Indian girl at this same location who was "as white as a Castilian lady" —probably fathered by one of the Spanish travelers.

Castañeda reported the second incident, which occurred on the expedition's return across the Great Plains from present-day Kansas.

Castañeda wrote that the expedition found a "painted" (tattooed) woman by herself on the plains along the Pecos River. Castañeda wrote she had escaped earlier as a slave of expeditionary Juan de Zaldivar. Castañeda reported she claimed to have been captured by "Spaniards who had entered the country from Florida to explore it in this direction." Castañeda wrote that he later learned that she said she ran away nine days earlier from other Spaniards. "She gave the names of some [Hernando de Soto] captains."[17] Nothing more is known about this woman whom Castañeda believed escaped from two Spanish expeditions.

* * *

Xauían remained in an unmarked grave or his bones lay bleached on a Moho battlefield. But Tiwas remembered him then as inspiration for rebelling

---

[17] Castañeda, *Journey of Coronado*, 77. Castañeda might have conflated identities of different women. He wrote about the incident more than twenty years later. He probably witnessed discovery of the woman, but perhaps he wrote hearsay told him years afterward about her time with Hernando de Soto's expedition. Did the Soto and Coronado expeditions almost meet?

against conquistadors representing one of the most powerful militaries of the 1500s in Europe.

Generations later the memory of Xauían faded. Today it is just historians, and only some of them, who remember the man by his Tiwa name.

Xauían was the first Native American leader to defy European invaders. His resistance in 1540–1541 was the first of America's official Indian Wars, which would go on for the next three hundred and seventy-seven years against both colonizing Spaniards and expanding Americans.

In the Battle of Bear Valley in Arizona on January 9, 1918, Yaquis fought a small engagement against US Army buffalo soldiers. The Battle of Bear Valley is now considered the final "official" battle of the "Indian Wars," which Xauían led in 1540-1541.

* * *

An investigation of Coronado and the way he conducted the expedition started soon after his return. Castañeda reported in another of his understatements that Viceroy Mendoza did not welcome Coronado "very graciously" upon the expedition's return.

Mendoza perhaps feared that finding his appointed general guilty would jeopardize his position as viceroy. In any case, Mendoza interceded in Coronado's investigation of war crimes, which led to Coronado's exoneration. But Coronado's second-in-command Cárdenas was convicted later in Spain on similar charges. Cárdenas's punishment after appeals was to serve a year in the king's army without pay along the Mediterranean coast, banishment from the Indies, and a fine of 200 ducats. The ducats fine was based on a gold currency common at that time throughout Europe. Although there's a wide range of estimates, the 200 ducats would be worth about $30,000 even then, and probably more today.

Historian Richard Flint concluded: "The punishment was largely symbolic for what were generally agreed to be horrendous crimes against American Natives. No one else was charged or tried."[18]

Converting Indians to the Catholic faith was the stated aim of almost every Spanish expedition of the sixteenth through eighteenth centuries. But there is little evidence of it in the Coronado chronicles.

It was an expedition officer, Hernando de Alvarado, not one of the Franciscan missionaries who accompanied Coronado, who wrote about one incident. He reported erection of tall crosses at Indian villages.

Alvarado wrote, "In the places where crosses were raised, we saw them worship these. They made offerings to these of their powder [paint] and feathers, and some left the blankets they had on. They showed so much zeal that some climbed up on the others to grasp the arms of the cross, to place feathers and flowers there, and others bringing ladders, while some held them, went up to tie strings, so as to fasten the flowers and the feathers."[19]

There might have been many unreported missionary attempts at the pueblos, but Castañeda mentioned none in his expedition account except some baptisms of children.

Franciscan Friar Marcos de Niza had gone with Coronado as a guide, but only as far as Hawikku. Coronado sent him back to Mexico City when he

---

[18] R. Flint, *No Settlement, No Conquest*, 241. There was discussion of bringing charges against Hernando de Alvarado, but that idea was dropped,

[19] "Narrative of Hernando Alvarado." Reprinted in Castañeda, *Journey of Coronado*, 244.

learned that Marcos had lied about riches at Cíbola.

Five other Franciscan friars reportedly went on Coronado's entire expedition. Three were ordained priests, and two were lay brothers. They were Fathers Juan de Padilla, Juan de la Croix, and Antonio de Castilblanco, plus Lay Brothers Luis de Úbeda, and Daniel (no surname).

Friar Padilla was the best known. He returned to Kansas in 1542 to be minister for Indians, but Plains Indians killed him there.[20] Memorials portray him as the first Christian martyr in what is now the United States. However, that first martyrdom is more appropriately valid for one of the three friars who died on the Narváez expedition to the Florida peninsula about fourteen years earlier. Úbeda went to Pecos Pueblo as a missionary and his fate is unknown. The rest went back to Mexico with Coronado.

Coronado has become a folk hero today to many Hispanics in the American Southwest. But he was not so favored at the end of the expedition by disillusioned Spaniards, including those who went on the expedition with him or officials in Mexico City.[21]

The *Real Audiencia* (Royal Audience) investigated Coronado, charging him with war crimes. Even though a sympathetic *Real Audiencia* court in Mexico City exonerated him, the Council of the Indies convicted his second-in-command Cárdenas on war crime charges in Spain afterward.

When Castañeda was full of enthusiasm for the

---

[20] When Friar Juan de Padilla opted to return to Kansas to minister to the Plains Indians, Historian Richard Flint observed, "Padilla must have considered his return to Quivira a glorious duty and a fortunate opportunity to hasten the return of Christ" in his millenarian belief. R. Flint, *No Settlement, No Conquest,* 8.

[21] R. Flint, *No Settlement, No Conquest.*

expedition, he wrote at its beginning that Coronado was "beloved and obeyed by his captains and soldiers as heartily as any of those who have ever started out in the Indies." But by early 1542 Castañeda's judgment changed. Castañeda wrote that Coronado's "power was slight, for he had been disobeyed already and was not much respected. He began to be afraid ... and kept a guard. ... And from this time on they did not obey the general as readily as formerly, and they did not show any affection for him."[22]

Coronado returned to Mexico City in disgrace because many of the expedition's investors—Viceroy Mendoza was the largest—were upset because he had cost them great sums of money and never found any riches. Even many resentful expedition members returned deep in debt, and Coronado lost much money.

One Spaniard testified at Coronado's investigation that he was a witness to the 1540 muster of members of Coronado's expedition going to the "Seven Cities" believes to start at the Zuni village of Cíbola/Hawikku. After praising several officers and key enlisted leaders of the "most splendid company," the witness to the muster roll opined:

"All the rest of the force were people without settled residences, who had recently come to the country in search of a living. It seemed to him that it was a very fortunate thing for Mexico that the people who were going [with Coronado] ... [for they] had been for the most part vicious young gentlemen, who did not have anything to do in the city or in the country. They were all going of their own free will and were very ready

---

[22] All of the paragraph's quotes are from Castañeda, *Journey of Coronado*. The quote at the beginning of the expedition is on page 118 and quotes toward the end of the expedition are on pages 131 and 122.

to help pacify [an early Spanish euphemism for "conquer"] the new country."[23]

Cristóbal de Oñate, a wealthy Spanish official who would be father of Juan de Oñate, New Mexico's colonizer more than a half-century later, was not impressed in reviewing the expedition's muster in February 1540, saying, "Many of those going were licentious and had no [means] by which to sustain themselves" in Mexico City or elsewhere.[24]

Historian Richard Flint maintained in his 2008 book, "Spaniards at the time commonly thought of the [Coronado] expedition as a shameful example of Christian conduct."[25]

Matías de la Mota Padilla, a 1700s Spanish historian, gave his reason for failure of the Coronado expedition, writing, "It was most likely the chastisement of God that riches were not found on this expedition, because, when this ought to have been the secondary object of the expedition, and the conversion of all those heathen their first aim, they bartered with fate and struggled after the secondary."[26]

Coronado died in 1554 of an unspecified disease in Mexico City at the age of 43 or 44. He was still in debt by 10,000 pesos after selling much of his property.

---

[23] R. Flint, *No Settlement, No Conquest*, 5. Many going on the expedition were members of a minor nobility class of Spaniards known as *hidalgos*.

[24] Ibid., 9.

[25] Ibid., 242.

[26] Day. "Mota Padilla on the Coronado Expedition," 105. Also on page 116 of Castañeda's account, the original 1896 translator George Parker Winship footnoted this criticism by historian Mota Padilla on the cause of the Coronado expedition's failure.

5 DIFFERENCES TODAY WITH 1500s

The sixteenth century presented a far different world from one that exists today.

Back then, nearly every society accepted slavery and other kinds of forced labor. Hammurabi drew up a law code for Babylon in about 1700 BC, which included rules on the proper treatment and use of slaves. Slavery was acknowledged in the Bible, and it was accepted in the United States until the thirteenth amendment to the Constitution in 1865. Slavery remained legal in several other countries, and forms of slavery still are acceptable today in some nations.

Enslavement of Indians was an early deliberate policy of colonists on the East Coast of what would become the United States. Slavery was intended to reduce the Indian population as well as to provide free labor. Some colonists deported Indians to slavery on the Caribbean Islands where there was no chance of return.

Slavery of Africans in what is now the US began seventy-seven years after Coronado in 1619. That's when a British pirate ship delivered twenty Africans to tobacco fields in colonial Virginia. At first those Africans were indentured servants. Later the status of the Africans was changed to perpetual slavery.[1]

It is only relatively recently that slavery has become unacceptable to most, after thousands of years of human enslavement across the globe. Slavery has been a common human condition of war captives and other natally alienated peoples in many cultures for thousands of years.

Forms of human slavery still exist. For example, prisoners still provide low wage labor for some corporations and in many states. Debt bondage remains accepted in many countries, and sex trafficking is common. Rebels in other countries use children as soldiers. Unpaid internships similar in some ways to indentured servitude are common in the US.

The "Doctrine of Discovery," which was repudiated by the Vatican in 2023, was a key motive for Spanish conquest in the sixteenth century. Under the doctrine, a more militarily advanced nation was permitted to invade and conquer any other civilization, enslave its people, and extract all resources for its own use. Researcher Stephen T. Newcomb wrote, "What is generally referred as the Doctrine of Discovery might be more accurately called ... the doctrine of Christian European invasion."[2]

Authorized by papal decrees in the 1400s, the doctrine was imposed by military forces against weaker civilizations from history's beginning. Although not known then by that name, it was practiced by the Roman Empire, Genghis Khan's horsemen warriors from Mongolia, Visigoths, Mongols from China

---

[1] Burr, *Complicated Lives* 201. Vermont was the first state to declare slavery illegal in 1777. An African American woman slave named Mumbet, who also was a Revolutionary War widow, won a lawsuit in 1783, which made slavery illegal in Massachusetts.

[2] Newcomb, Steven T. *Pagans in the Promised Land*, 94. Quoted in Charles, Mark, and Soong-Chan Rah. *The Ongoing, Dehumanizing Legacy,* 70.

invading eastern Europe in the thirteenth and fourteen centuries, etc.

The papal decrees gave that policy the name of Doctrine of Discovery.

Europeans used forced labor and slavery for subjugating Natives throughout Africa, the Caribbean, and Mexico, as well as North, Central, and South America in the sixteenth and seventeenth centuries.[3] The Catholic Church authorized slavery of non-Christians, and the New World's gold and silver was needed to finance the Spanish royalty's continuing wars in the sixteenth century. According to Wikipedia, Spain fought nineteen wars against major European powers including the Ottoman Empire in the 1500s.

It is a major misconception, however, that finding gold and silver was the original reason for the Coronado expedition being sent north from Mexico in 1540–1542 into what is now the United States.[4] At least it wasn't the main reason until Coronado became disappointed at the subsistence-level occupants and the dried mud appearance of Hawikku at the "Seven Cities of Cíbola."

The main reason for sending Coronado north was to find a land route to Greater India and China for the world's most sought-after luxuries of silk, porcelain, spices, and dyes, plus other trading goods. The Ottoman Empire blocked Europeans from traveling to the Far East by land. But at that time it was thought that there was a land connection north or west of Mexico to the Far East.[5]

But that little knowledge of geography ruined their

---

[3] R. Flint, *No Settlement, No Conquest*, 6, 15.

[4] Ibid., xv.

[5] Ibid., 18, 19, 21.

plan. It was for good reason that Europeans called the joined continents of the Americas "The New World," because none had traveled to there before. Their lack of knowing geographic details was like the ignorance of geography details today about never-visited planets and moons in Earth's solar system.

Castañeda wrote conventional wisdom about the Far East more than twenty years after the expedition. "I will now tell ... what direction the army took, and the direction in which Greater India lies, which was what they pretended to be in search of." He wrote in the 1560s, "Since we were in the north, we ought to have turned to the west (his presumed land route toward Greater India and China) instead of toward the east as we did."[6] Castañeda had insisted earlier, "This land of [Mexico] is part of the mainland with Peru, and with Greater India or China as well."[7]

Castañeda's sixteenth century misunderstanding of world geography continued: "[Coronado] preferred, however, to follow the reports of the Turk, but it would have been better to cross the mountains where this river [Rio Grande] rises. I believe they would have ... reached the lands from which these people started, which from its location is on the edge of Greater India."[8]

Columbus's religious faith taught there were only three continents—Europe, Asia, and Africa. Columbus knew the Earth was round, but he underestimated Earth's size when his ships encountered the Caribbean Islands in 1492. Europeans didn't realize the Caribbean Islands were far short of Greater India, nor that the

[6] Castañeda, *Journey of Coronado*, 134–135.

[7] Ibid., 83.

[8] Ibid., 108–109.

joined landmass that became known as the Americas was a previously unknown continent.

Columbus's religious upbringing and his underestimation of Earth's size combined to make Columbus think that the Caribbean Islands were near Greater India. So he referred to Natives there as *indios*, a Spanish word that continues today in English as Indians.

A primary motivation for colonists in Mexico to join early expeditions was to find wealth in unexplored lands. Expedition members hoped to establish lucrative encomienda estates, where they could get rich using forced labor/slavery of Indians and receiving Indian tribute (a form of taxation).[9] Conquistadors assumed that such encomiendas would be similar to Indians working on such forced-labor estates in the Caribbean Islands and in Mexico. However, instead of millions of Indians living in Mexico, the Pueblo Indians to the north numbered only in the thousands. There just weren't enough Indians available to grant profitable encomiendas to Coronado's many expeditionaries who hoped to establish one.[10]

A Dominican friar, Antonio de Montesinos, was the first European to denounce the abuse, enslavement, and killing of Indians. He outraged owners of encomiendas and Spanish officials in Cuba when he delivered a church sermon in 1511 that denounced that times' Spanish system of warfare and using forced labor/slavery on encomienda estates and mines.

Listing injustices, which he said were mortal sins, Montesinos asked: "Tell me by what right of justice do you hold these Indians in such a cruel and horrible

---

[9] "Tribute provided to encomenderos generally took the form of labor." R. Flint, *No Settlement, No Conquest*, 6.

[10] Ibid., 5.

servitude? On what authority have you waged such detestable wars against these people who dwelt quietly and peacefully on their own lands? Wars in which you have destroyed such an infinite number of them by homicides and slaughters never heard of before. Why do you keep them so oppressed and exhausted, without giving them enough to eat or curing them of the sicknesses they incur from the excessive labor you give them, and they die, or rather you kill them, in order to extract and acquire gold every day."[11]

That sermon infuriated most Spaniards, but inspired another Catholic Dominican Order friar, Bartolomé de las Casas, who was present. He campaigned for the last five decades of his life at the Vatican and courts of Spanish kings Ferdinand II and Carlos I against the encomiendas, mines, and other abuse of Indians.

Las Casas became "Protector of the Indians," a role that made him a hero to indigenous people and other Dominicans. But it aroused fierce opposition from colonists. Las Casas favored gentle conversion.

Las Casas's campaign resulted in the "New Laws of the Indies for the Good Treatment and Preservation of the Indians," issued in 1542. The New Laws set in motion the phasing out of encomiendas and banned Indian slavery. Colonists on the other side of the Atlantic Ocean in the Americas found ways around the New Laws. They would continue abuses against tribes for some time afterward. Regardless, Spain was the first nation to ban Indian slavery.

Although the New Laws mostly predated the Coronado expedition, they might have contributed to charges against Coronado. His conduct seemed in

---

[11] Sanderlin, *Witness*, 66-67. Also, R. Flint, *No Settlement, No Conquest*, 30, 66, 237-239. Also Herrick, *Esteban: The African Slave*, 224n2 and 225n24.

defiance of the New Laws. Official testimonies started in 1544 at Mexico City and continued into 1546.

There also were religious reasons for conquering and converting Indians. Franciscan friars who were missionaries to Indians believed conversion of Natives in the Americas would bring on the second coming of Jesus Christ in their lifetime.[12] They believed that the Messiah would rule for a millennium and then the world would end. Catholics espousing that view into the 1500s were known as millenarians. Historian Richard Flint noted, "All sixteen of the Franciscan missionaries to [Mexico] … were millenarians, as was the first bishop of Mexico, Fray Juan de Zumárraga."[13]

The Catholic Church later declared millenarianism to be an errant doctrine.

Flint wrote: "Decisive were the sudden and widespread deaths of so many Indian people. …. The shock of a death rate [from disease, war, and forced labor/slavery] of perhaps one-third was profound. … Some friars saw the deaths as a divine message that their single-minded, urgent project of conversion was misguided. … Successors to the millenarian missionaries were more often friars who looked with disfavor on the old apocalyptic school of evangelism."[14]

Nevertheless, up through the Coronado expedition the millenarian belief motivated Franciscan friars to encourage conquest as well as conversion of survivors.

Franciscan millenarian missionaries believed force was justified against non-Catholics. Therefore,

---

[12] Phelan, *The Millennial Kingdom.*

[13] R. Flint, *No Settlement, No Conquest*, 8. Zumárraga is the bishop linked with the vision of Our Lady of Guadalupe near Mexico City in December of 1531.

[14] Ibid, 224.

millenarianism and racism might have combined to influence some conquistadors and colonists to justify mass killing of Indians.

After Coronado's first war, the North American continent continued to be aflame with wars against the original Native inhabitants of what is now the United States.

By the third decade of the 1800s, the Eastern tribes had been decimated by war, disease, bounties, slaves sold to the Caribbean, or confined to small reservations.

An exception was the "Five Civilized Tribes" who occupied prime agricultural land in Southern states.[15]

Today, many ruins of ancient Indian pueblos warred against at the start of the Indian Wars are close to Albuquerque, within or near areas traveled by the Coronado expedition in 1540–42.

Pecos Pueblo is now the site of Pecos National Historical Park (visitor center and gift shop), and Kuaua Pueblo is now partially restored with a museum and gift shop at the Coronado Historic Site near Bernalillo. Other restored or original historical sites at or near Coronado's travels in New Mexico are Bandelier National Monument near Los Alamos (ruins, museum and gift shop), Salinas Pueblo Missions National Monument (three pueblo ruins), Ácoma Pueblo

---

[15] In 1830, President Andrew Jackson ordered the US Army to force Southeastern tribes to move to Oklahoma west of the Mississippi River. Although the Cherokee are most identified with the "Trail of Tears," the long walk also included the Chickasaw, Choctaw, Creek, and Seminole tribes. Hundreds died on the long forced trip, especially babies and the elderly. Meskwaki Indians also were moved out of Iowa. Then the Manifest Destiny wars against Western Indians continued for nearly a hundred years. National Poet Laureate Joy Harjo imagined her Creek ancestors in *An American Sunrise*, xv, seeing white settlers moving into their former homes with "guns, Bibles, household goods, families, taking what had been ours, as we were surrounded by soldiers and driven away like livestock at gunpoint."

(museum and mesa-top tours of pueblo buildings), Zuni Pueblo (visitors center and gift shop, tours), Jemez National Historic Landmark in Jemez Springs (pueblo ruins, museum and gift shop), and Petroglyph National Monument (museum, original Indian and Spanish petroglyphs on rocks) at Albuquerque.

In 1540 many pueblos existed along the Rio Grande, in the Galisteo Basin south of Santa Fe, and on both sides of the Sandia and Manzano mountain ranges.

There are many historic Indian pueblo ruins throughout New Mexico. Many exist because a scarcity of water in much of the Southwest has prevented development that would build over many historic sites.

Mountains still rise like crooked blue shadows in every direction in what is now the state of New Mexico where Coronado traveled.

High above the desert, the mountains intercept rain to nourish forests of ponderosa pines, pastures, and waterfalls. Bears, cougars, deer, and elk still roam there.

As late as October 1999, a Sandia Pueblo man wrote an account in English of visiting two secret ancient shrine sites in the Sandia Mountains. He still was a devoted follower of his Puebloan ancestors' religion of kivas and katsinas. The man offered a pinch of cornmeal at each shrine and said his prayers to the Creator.[16]

---

[16] "Journey to the Sacred Mountain." The author of this book did not realize sacred shrine sites remained in remote mountain regions that followers of ancient Native religions still visited. He was astonished to read such a recent account of the Sandia Pueblo man. Now it's known that many such sacred shrines still exist and are visited by Natives who observe their original Native religion, although they might also attend Christian churches, seeing no conflict to praying to the Creator in different religions

6 MODERN ERA

For hundreds of years after the Tiguex War, the ruin of Ghufoor Pueblo melted into the earth under the New Mexico sun, rains, and wind. With each decade, walls collapsed and memories dimmed of Xauían's home pueblo and Coronado's headquarters.

In June 1934 a crew of archaeologists, students, and laborers appeared with shovels, pickaxes, and trucks at the old site of Ghufoor Pueblo on the west side of the Rio Grande, across from today's Bernalillo, New Mexico. They began digging, first at the Ghufoor site, then at the site of Kuaua Pueblo, two miles northeast of Ghufoor. Both ancient pueblos lay at the edge of windy, sunny desert bluffs overlooking the Rio Grande, and both were on the west side of the river.

About six hundred skeletons were exhumed at Kuaua.[1] Hundreds of burials also were excavated at Ghufoor Pueblo, which is the site now known as Santiago. Many skeletons are in storage at the osteology department at the University of New Mexico, and photographs of some skeletons are in museums. Such massive excavation of Native graves without reburial was common in archaeology of the time, despite

---

[1] Sinclair, *The Story of the Pueblo of Kuaua,* 10.

Puebloans still living nearby.

Burials under the floors of rooms at Kuaua were primarily children and childbirth-age women.[2] This was true also at Santiago. Other burials at both pueblos were found in the plazas or outside the pueblo walls.

In 1999–2013, volunteers from Friends of Coronado Historic Site conducted a multi-year project of photographing and cataloguing artifacts recovered from Kuaua and Santiago. Many had been stored and not seen since the 1930s. The volunteers discovered that some artifacts from Santiago and Kuaua were co-mingled, mislabeled, carelessly packaged, lent or gifted by Hewett to institutions and friends, or lost.

All excavated at Ghufoor, and now at the Museum of New Mexico, the canteen with its water symbols shows how a shape can be created identically even in different civilizations. The pottery above shows unidentified symbols at left and what could be images of dragonflies at right.

Excavations continued in the 1930s at the Ghufoor and Kuaua sites. Attention focused on Kuaua because its excavation discovered pre-columbian mural paintings of Puebloan figures, katsinas, and cultural scenes on one kiva's walls.

Discovery of the murals turned ever more attention to Kuaua. The village was partially restored by

---

2 Ethan Ortega, then a ranger at Coronado Historic Site, in presentation about new discoveries at Kuaua Pueblo, January 15, 2017.

uncovering the foundations to its ground walls, rooms, and five kivas to make its ruin part of Coronado Historic Site. Then the original walls were back-filled to protect them. Mud bricks in the Spanish style were built atop the original walls to show the size and location of the ground floor rooms. Excavation of both pueblos was so loosely supervised by archaeologist Edgar L. Hewett that many recovered artifacts were mislabeled for decades, given away by Hewett to friends, and distributed among museums. Although artifacts such as katsina head covers and stone sculptures were found at other contemporary pueblos' excavations, none were reported at Kuaua or Santiago. For another example, hundreds of arrowheads were found at other pueblo excavations, but only about a dozen were found originally at Hewett's two pueblos. Collectors prized arrowheads, and most are believed to have left the sites of Kuaua and Ghufoor pueblos in the pockets of students and local excavation workers. Some artifacts might never have been spotted because photographs show workers throwing shovelfuls of dirt aside in their haste to uncover original walls. As a result, Kuaua and Ghufoor were not admitted to the federal system of archaeological sites, and only Kuaua is part of the New Mexico's Coronado Historic Site.

Ghufoor originally was part of the Coronado Historic Site. But Hewett became convinced that Kuaua was more important, and he wasn't aware that Ghufoor Pueblo had been Coronado's headquarters for two winters. The state relinquished to private ownership the site of Ghufoor (identified since 1702 on a Spanish map as Santiago Pueblo). That site later was obliterated after excavation by quarrying for gravel underneath it. The original site of Ghufoor/Coofor/Santiago now is covered by a housing development known as

"Santiago."

Kuaua's kiva murals are among the finest pre-columbian Native mural paintings in what is now the United States. In 1938, Zia artist Ma Pe Wi painted reproductions of murals from some of the seventeen layers on the walls of one restored kiva. Constance Silver restored his fresco murals in 2002. Some excavated originals are displayed at the Coronado Historic Site and others are stored in museums. The mural paintings of katsinas and Puebloan culture would have been familiar to Xauían and generations of Tiwas.

The original Ghufoor site might have rivaled Kuaua as a tourist attraction in New Mexico, if it had survived, because it was Coronado's headquarters known as Coofor in the winters of 1540–41 and 1541–42. A private landowner bulldozed the ancient pueblo in the 1950s to sell the gravel it was built on. Its historical value was further diminished when houses were built over and on three sides of the Ghufoor site in the 1990s.

This 2017 photo showing deterioration of "restored" walls in the northwest corner of Kuaua Pueblo 70 years after restoration work of ground floor rooms and walls. It proves what weather can do to dried mud pueblo structures even after a few decades.

The original site of Ghufoor Pueblo is difficult to find because a New Mexico Historic Marker identifying it is about a quarter of a mile south and on the opposite side of the NM 528 highway. The marker's inscription is: "Spanish Entrada Site—Among the many prehistoric and historic sites nearby is a camp where Francisco de Vasquez [sic] de

Coronado's troops may have spent the 1540–41 winter. Coronado also visited the ancient pueblo of Kuaua located to the north. Kuaua's ruins are partially restored and interpreted at the Coronado Historic Monument [sic] near Bernalillo."

* * *

Some might claim Hernando de Soto fought the first Indian war in July 1539 in Florida when his force waged a battle against a Florida tribe. He and his men in the ensuing three years fought several other Southeastern tribes from the Gulf of Mexico up to Arkansas.

But Soto's battles with diverse tribes across more than four thousand miles is considered to be just a series of raids as he moved on to fight each different tribe. His expedition wandered through ten present-day Southern states in a search for European-style riches he could plunder.

However, Coronado waged an official "declared war" against one tribe (at that time the Tigua, but now the Tiwa).

Therefore, Coronado's action has been recognized as the first *named and declared* war in what is now the United States against Native Americans. Even though many battles costing the lives of Europeans and Native Americans were fought earlier, the Tiguex War was the first fought for dominance, ruling authority, and control over one tribe, the Tiwa people. For that reason, the Tiguex War is the first of America's Indian Wars, which would continue for possession of the North American continent for nearly four centuries.

Fatality estimates from history are difficult, but they are especially problematic for the Coronado expedition, with figures reported by only one source—Castañeda. He estimated that more than four hundred Indians were killed at Hawikku and the Tiguex pueblos, as well as twenty-one Europeans. Indian deaths might have been significantly higher. Even using Castañeda's conservative estimates, the Tiwas suffered deaths in excess of 10 percent of their population

Relying on Castañeda for information as the most thorough chronicler of the Coronado expedition leaves a lot of room for speculation and even fiction and folklore.[4] *America's First Indian War* attempts to focus on facts from many sources.

--A Harvest of Reluctant Souls: Fray Alonso de Benavides's History of New Mexico,1630.

This photograph was taken in 1912 of mounds in the foreground that marked the collapsed and not yet excavated ruin of Ghufoor Pueblo, in front of and across the Rio Grande from Sandia Mountain. It shows how Ghufoor Pueblo (Coronado's commandeered pueblo for his headquarters) and also Kuaua appeared before excavation in the twentieth century. Sandia Mountain is five miles distant.

Two Tiguex pueblos—Isleta and Sandia—along with seventeen other pueblos in New Mexico have persevered under foreign powers. All still maintain much of their ancient culture.

The Indian Pueblo Cultural Center at 2401 12th Street NW in Albuquerque (https://indianpueblo.org) includes a museum, library, archives, gift shop, and

4 Herrick. "The Tiguex War in Fact, Folklore, and Fiction." Flint and Flint. *The Latest Word*, 425-438.

commercial enterprises including a restaurant as well as Puebloan dance performances, art, historical displays, and cultural programming. Feast Day celebrations are open to the public at individual pueblos. The center is administered by the All Pueblo Council of Governors, which has existed under different names since the 1700s. The council is a nonprofit leadership organization and political entity representing the nineteen modern pueblos in New Mexico on legislative, cultural, and governmental issues.

Charles F. Lummis lived at Isleta Pueblo from 1888 to 1892, and in ca. 1912 excavated part of a wall at Kuaua.[5] He reported in 1927 that the original Tiwa name for either Ghufoor/Coofor/Santiago or Kuaua might have been *T'ur-jai-ai* or *Tur-jui-ai*. It's not certain which pueblo he referred to. Lummis's translation of the Tiwa name meant "Sun Coming Up Place."

Indeed, the sunrise coming up over Sandia Mountain at either pueblo site can be spectacular.

Few books have been written about the Tiguex War of 1540–1541.[6]

---

[5] Sinclair, *The Story of the Pueblo of Kuaua,* 19.

[6] Xauían is a major historical character in Herrick's 2013 historical novel *Winter of the Metal People,* which presents the Pueblo Indian point of view about the Coronado expedition and the Tiguex War. A historian's detailed 2008 account of the war and Coronado expedition is *No Settlement, No Conquest* by Richard L. Flint.

BIBLIOGRAPHY

Barrett, Elinore, M. *Conquest and Catastrophe: Changing Rio Grande Pueblo Settlement Patterns in the Sixteenth and Seventeenth Centuries* (Albuquerque: University of New Mexico Press, 2002).

Castañeda, Pedro de, of Nájera. *The Journey of Coronado,* Trans. and ed. by George Parker Winship (Washington, D.C.: Bureau of Ethnology 14th Annual Report, 1896. Repr. (New York: A.S. Barnes, 1904).

Charles, Mark, and Soong-Chan Rah *The Ongoing, Dehumanizing Legacy of the Doctrine of Discovery* (Madison, WI: IVP, imprint of InterVarsity Press, 2019).

Chavez, Rev. Angélico, "Coronado's Friars." *Hispanic American Historical Review,* (1969, 49 (4)..

Cobus, Rubén. *A Dictionary of New Mexico and Southern Colorado Spanish* (Santa Fe: Museum of New Mexico Press, 1983).

Coze, Paul. "Kachinas: Masked Dancers of the Southwest" in *National Geographic.* 112, no. 2 (August 1957).

Davis, W.W.H. *The Spanish Conquest of New Mexico* (Doylestown, PA.: 1869).

Day, A. Grove, "Mota Padilla on the Coronado Expedition," *Hispanic American Historical Review,* 20:1. (1939) Reprinted by Duke University Press

Diamond, Jared. *Guns, Germs, and Steel* (New York: W.W. Norton & Co., 2017).

Fisher, Reginald G. "Second Report of the Archaeological Survey of the Pueblo Plateau" in *Santa Fe Sub-Quadrangle,* vol.1, No. 1, *The University of New Mexico Bulletin,* plat 7 (July 1, 1931).

Flint, Richard. "Without Them, Nothing was Possible: The Coronado Expedition's Indian Allies," *New Mexico Historical Review,* 84:1 (Winter 2009).

Flint, Richard. *No Settlement, No Conquest: A History of the Coronado Entrada* (Albuquerque: University of New Mexico Press, 2008).

Flint, Richard. *Great Cruelties Have Been Reported: The 1544 Investigation of the Coronado Expedition* (Albuquerque: University of New Mexico Press, 2002).

Flint, Richard. "Moho and the Tiguex War," a chapter in *The Latest Word from 1540: People, Places, and Portrayals of the Coronado Expedition* (Albuquerque: University of New Mexico Press, 2011).

Flint, Richard, and Shirley Cushing Flint. "Castañeda de Nájera's Narrative" chapter in *Documents of the Coronado*

Expedition, 1539-1542 (Albuquerque: University of New Mexico Press, 2012).

Flint, Richard, and Shirley Cushing Flint, eds. *A Most Splendid Company: The Coronado Expedition In Global Perspective* (Albuquerque: University of New Mexico Press, 2019).

Flint, Richard and Shirley Cushing Flint. "A Remarkable Memory of a bridge built by the Coronado Expedition," *New Mexico Historical Review.* Vol. 98, Number 1. Winter 2023.

Folsom, Franklin. *Red Power on the Rio Grande* (New York: Simon & Schuster, 2005).

Gibson, Daniel. *Pueblos of the Rio Grande* (Rio Nuevo Publishers, Tucson, AZ, 2001, 2011).

Hämäläinen, Pekka. *Indigenous Continent: The Epic Contest for North America* (New York: Liveright Publishing Corporation [W.W. Norton & Co.] 2022).

Hammond, George P., and Agapito Rey. *Narratives of the Coronado Expedition, 1540–1542* (Albuquerque: University of New Mexico Press, 1940).

Harjo, Joy. *An American Sunrise* (New York: W.W. Norton & Company, 2019).

Herrick, Dennis. *Winter of the Metal People: The Untold Story of America's First Indian War* (Mechanicsburg, PA: Sunbury Press Inc., 2013).

Herrick, Dennis. "Xauían and the Tiguex War." *Native Peoples* magazine (January-February 2014) Vol. 27, No. 1.

Herrick, Dennis. "The Tiguex War in fact, folklore, and fiction," chapter in *The Latest Word from 1540: People, Places, and Portrayals of the Coronado Expedition* (Albuquerque: University of New Mexico Press, 2011).

Herrick, Dennis. "The Indian Who Defied Coronado." (Rio Rancho, NM: Sterling Publications USA, 2014).

Herrick, Dennis. *Faded Pueblos of the Tiguex War.* (Rio Rancho, NM: Sterling Publications USA, 2017–2023).

Hewett, Edgar L., and Wayne L. Mauzy. *Landmarks of New Mexico* (Albuquerque: University of New Mexico Press, 1940).

Ivey, James E, Diane Lee Rhodes, and Joseph P. Sanchez. "A special history report prepared for the Coronado Trail Study," National Park Service.

Kessell, John L. *Kiva, Cross, and Crown* (Washington, DC: National Park Service, 1979).

Ladd, Edmund J. "Zuni On the Day the Men in Metal Arrived," chapter in Richard Flint and Shirley Cushing Flint. *The Coronado Expedition to Tierra Nueva: The 15400–1542 Route Across the Southwest* (Denver: University Press of

Colorado, 1997).

Lauriano, Andres. "Journey to the Sacred Mountain," reprint of 1999 article. *Pueblo of Sandia Newsletter*, Vol 3 No. 3 (summer 2002), 1 and 4.

Lummis, Charles F., letter to Dr. Edgar L. Hewett at the School of American Research (July 13, 1927).

Mathers, Clay. "The grammar and syntax of battle: Kuaua Pueblo, the Pueblo de la Cruz, and constructing analytical frameworks for the Tiguex War (1540–1542)," in *A Lifelong Journey: Papers in honor of Michael P. Marshall*. Vol. 46 (Albuquerque: Archaeological Society of New Mexico, 2020).

Morrow, Baker H. *A Harvest of Reluctant Souls*: *Fray Alonso de Benavides's History of New Mexico, 1630* (Denver: University Press of Colorado, 1996).

Phelan, John Leddy. *The Millennial Kingdom of the Franciscans in the New World* (Berkeley, CA: University of California Press, 1970).

Riley, Carroll L. *Rio del Norte: People of the Upper Rio Grande from Earliest Times to the Pueblo Revolt (*Salt Lake City: University of Utah Press, 1995).

Riley, Carroll L. *The Kachina and the Cross: Indians and Spaniards in the Early Southwest* (Salt Lake City: University of Utah Press, 1999).

Roberts, David. *The Pueblo Revolt* (New York: Simon & Schuster, 2005).

Schmader, Matthew F., "New Light on the Francisco Vázquez de Coronado Expedition of 1540–1542," in Biannual Southwest Symposium, January 2010.

Sinclair,John. *The Story of the Pueblo of Kuaua* (Whitefish, MT: Literary Licensing, 2012).

Newcomb, Steven T. *Pagans in the Promised Land: Decoding the Doctrine of Christian Discovery* (Golden, CO: Fulcrum Publishing: 2008).

Sanderlin, George, ed. and trans. *Witness: Writing of Bartolomé de las Casas* (Maryknoll, NY: Orbis, 1971).

Sando, Joe S. *Pueblo Nations: Eight Centuries of Pueblo Indian History* (Santa Fe: Clear Light Publishing, 1992).

Sando, Joe S. and Herman Agoyo. *Po'pay: Leader of the First American Revolution* (Santa Fe: Clear Light Publishing, 2005).

Simmons, Marc. "Coronado blunder," *Santa Fe New Mexican* (May 8, 2010), A-8,

Tello, Antonio. *Libro Segundo de la Crónicas Miscelánea* (Guadalajara, Mexico: La República Literaria, 1891).

Tichy, Marjorie Ferguson. "The Archaeology of Puaray."

(Albuquerque, NM: *El Palacio*, 1939) 46:7.

Waters, Frank. *Brave Are My People: Indian Heroes Not Forgotten* (Santa Fe: Clear Light Publishing, 1993).

Wood, Michael. *Conquistadors* (Berkeley: University of California Press, 2000).

Major Indian Wars and Battles

Thousands of Indians were killed in intertribal wars even after the first Europeans arrived on the continent.

But smallpox was the greatest ally that Europeans ever had. Indians had no immunity to the disease. The disease erupted out of Massachusetts in 1633. Within eight years, half of all Indians died of smallpox from New England to Chesapeake Bay. In many villages, every Native died. The fatality rate in New England was 80 percent. Smallpox killed thousands more Indians over the following years.

There was fighting between nearly all the major events by Native tribes against colonists from Spain, Netherlands, Great Britain, France, Russia, and elsewhere, and finally by the US Army. This is a partial list of major Indian wars and battles over four centuries, when fighting was nearly continuous inside what is now the United States, steadily reducing Native population.

Clashes predating America's "Indian Wars" period

Ponce de León vs the Calusa (FL) —1513, 1517, 1521
Spanish claim to Florida — 1513-1763, 1783-1818
Allyón colonization attempt (Georgia) — 1526
Pánfilo de Narváez expedition (Florida) — 1528
Hernando de Soto expedition — 1539-43
    Napituca Massacre (FL) — 1539
    Battle of Mabila (Alabama) — 1540

America's "Indian Wars" period

Coronado vs Puebloans, Tiguex War (NM) — 1540-42
Spanish sail into San Diego Harbor (CA) — 1542
Spanish colonization of New Mexico — 1592-1680
Acoma Massacre (NM) — 1599
Beaver Wars (Iroquois vs other tribes) — 1609-1701
Powhatan wars — 1609-14, 1622-26, 1644-46

Spanish build Palace of Governors (NM) — 1610
Pequot War — 1636-37
Kieft's War — 1643-45
Peach Tree War — 1655
Esopus wars — 1659-60, 1663-64
Battle of Long Sault — 1660
King Philip's War — 1675-76
First Pueblo Revolt — 1680
French colonization of Texas — 1684-89
King William's War — 1689-97
Spanish reconquest of New Mexico — 1692-1821
Second Pueblo Revolt — 1696
Fox Wars — 1701-42
Queen Anne's War — 1702-13
Spanish build Palace of Governors (NM) — 1610
Ute/Comanche mounted raids (NM) — 1710s-1762
Tuscarora War — 1711-15
Yamassee War — 1715-17
Spanish colonization of Texas — 1716-1821
Comanche mounted raids (NM) — 1719-1786
French/Pawnee vs Spanish/Pueblo (NE) — 1720
Lipan Apache battles (TX) — 1720s-1749
Drummer's War — 1722-25
King George's War —1744-48
Battle of Fort Necessity — 1754
French & Indian War (tribal coalition)— 1754-63
Gen. Edward Braddock's defeat — 1755
Anglo-Cherokee War — 1758-61
Cherokee Uprising — 1760-62
Pontiac's Rebellion (tribal coalition) — 1763-66
Lord Dunmore's War — 1774
Western Theater of the Revolution — 1775-83
Twenty Years War vs Shawnee — 1775-95
Cherokee-American wars — 1776-94, 1786-95
Spanish build Tucson Presidio (AZ) — 1777
Chickasaw-American War — 1780-81
Northwest War (Ohio, Ind., Ill., Mich.) — 1785-95
Logan's Raid vs Shawnee villages — 1786
Harmer Campaign vs Miamis & Shawnee — 1790
Gen. Arthur St. Clair's defeat —1791
Fallen Timbers battle — 1794
Nickajack expedition — 1794
Russian-Indian War (Alaska) — 1802-05
Sabine expedition — 1806
Tippecanoe battle — 1811
Tecumseh's Rebellion — 1811-13

War of 1812 — 1812-15
Peoria War — 1813
Creek War — 1813-14
Battle of Horseshoe Bend — 1814
First Seminole War (FL)— 1816-18
Comanche Wars (primarily vs Mexico) — 1821-70
Winnebago War (Wisconsin) — 1827
Black Hawk War — 1832
Second Seminole War (FL)—1835-42
Jicarilla War (NM) — 1849-55
Third Seminole War — 1855-58

Indian wars west of Mississippi River

Arikara War — 1823

Texas-Indian wars — 1820-77
Osage War — 1837
Comanche Great Raid (Texas) — 1840
  (Cholera/smallpox decimate Comanches — 1847
Cayuse War — 1847-55
Ute wars — 1849-55
Apache wars — 1849-86
Wakara's War (Utah) — 1853-54
Battle of Cieneguilla — 1854
Rogue River War — 1855-56
Tintic War (Utah)— 1856-60s
Antelope Hills expedition — 1858
Chiricahua War — 1861-72
Dakota War — 1862
Kit Carson campaign vs Navajos — 1863
Colorado War vs several tribes — 1863-65
Cheyenne War — 1864
Sand Creek Massacre (Colorado)— 1864
First Battle of Adobe Walls — 1864
Sheridan's campaign — 1868-75
Camp Grant Massacre — 1871
Yavapai War — 1871-75
Second Battle of Adobe Walls — 1874
Red River War — 1874-75
Nez Pearce War — 1877
Buffalo Hunters' War — 1877

Siouan Wars

Grattan Fight — 1854
First Sioux War — 1854-56
Dakota Sioux Uprising (Minnesota) — 1862

Sibley campaign — 1863
Sully campaign — 1864
Battle of Julesburg — 1865
Powder River War — 1865
Red Cloud's War (tribal coalition) — 1866-68
Fetterman Fight — 1866
Yellowstone expedition — 1874
Great Sioux War — 1876-77
Battle of the Little Bighorn — 1876
Miles campaigns — 1876-77
Ghost Dance massacre (Wounded Knee) — 1890

More wars west of the Mississippi River

Apache raids vs Mexicans & colonists —1831-50
Mexico bounty on Apache scalps (AZ) — 1835–46
California Indian wars — 1850s-80
Mangas Colorados raids (AZ) — 1851–62
Puget Sound War — 1855-56
Winnas Expedition (Oregon) — 1855
Yakima War (vs several tribes) — 1855-58
Battle of Seattle — 1856
Coeur d'Alene War — 1858
Mohave War — 1858
Paiute War — 1860
Snake War (northwestern states) — 1864-68
Hualapai War — 1865-70
Modoc War — 1872-73
Nez Perce War (Western states) — 1877
Bannock War (Idaho & Oregon) — 1878
Big Horn Sheepeater Indian War — 1879
Cochise Apache wars —1862–72
Geronimo's campaign —1877-86
Victorio's War (Texas & Mexico)— 1879-80
Nana & Geronimo Apache raids (AZ) — 1881–86
Crow War — 1887
Continuing Apache raids (AZ) — until 1890
US invasion of Hawaii (queen dethroned) — 1893
Wilcox Rebellion (Hawaii) — 1895
Yaqui Uprising (mainly vs Mexico) — 1896-1929
Bear Valley battle (Yaquis vs 10th Cavalry) — 1918

Official End of America's "Indian Wars"

However, Utah settlers quelled a 1923 rebellion by Utes and
Paiutes in 1923.

———Index———

unclear if Coronado present during atrocities, 50; aerial photo of possible site, 38; never excavated, 38

Montesinos, Antonio de: first protest against Indian abuses, 78–79

Narváez, Panfilo de: led Florida expedition, 68; four travelers, 65

Nahuatl: language of Aztecs and trade language, 55

Padilla, Juan de, friar: went as missionary to Quivira, 71; falsely named as first US Christian martyr, 70

Pecos Pueblo: battle at, 61

Pedreo cannons: apparently fired at Hawikku, 16, 61; maybe at Ghufoor & Arenal, 46; not at Moho, 46; Zia Pueblo takes custody, 61

Piedras Marcadas Pueblo: mentioned, 13, 50; expedition attacks, 52

Pueblo de la Cruz: perhaps second besieged pueblo, 43, 53–55

Pueblo Revolt of 1680: 37

Piedras Marcadas Pueblo: Tiguex village, 14; attacked, 55

Puaray Pueblo: Tiguex

Pueblo, 14; mistakenly identified, 22; never excavated, 38

Quivira, pronouncer, 22; Coronado leads expedition onto Plains, 18; Kansas, 22-23;

rape: at Arenal, 28–28; 33

requerimiento: end text, 40

Rio Grande: names, 7

Sandia Pueblo: one of two surviving Southern Tiwa speaking pueblos, 9; 26; 36; 85–86

Sandia Mountain: location, 11; "Watermelon Mountain," 11; sanctuary, 36; Sandia man to sacred site, 82; photo of, 89

Santa Ana Pueblo: relocate, 10

Santa Ana Mesa: possible site of Moho, 40, 52

San Felipe Pueblo: did not exist in Coronado's time, 10; near possible Moho site, 52

Santiago Pueblo: See Ghufoor Pueblo

Santiago housing development, 85

Santiago! : conquistador

From the Author

This is an expanded version of an article in *Native People's* magazine in 2014 titled, "Xauian and the Tiguex War." The book's map and photographs are by Dennis Herrick unless otherwise credited. Special thanks to premier Coronado scholars Richard Flint and Shirley Cushing Flint. To paraphrase quotations researcher John Bartlett: "I have collected flowers from many historians, and nothing but the tie that binds them is mine." Any error or misinterpretation in these pages is my fault alone.

Dennis Herrick is author of several short stories, often featuring different tribes of Puebloan Indians. As of 2023, he is the author of more than twenty-five 99-cent short stories and the following books. His author's website is at dennisherrick.com

Books by Dennis Herrick

Esteban: The African Slave Who Explored America
Winter of the Metal People
Missionaries from the Stars
A Brother's Cold Case
War of the Planet Burners
Faded Pueblos of the Tiguex War
Guest Bedroom: Collected Stories (20 short stories)
Pueblo Mysteries (6 short stories)
Newspaper Stories (8 short stories and 2 novel excerpts)
Farewell to the Master (Annotated reprint)
First Contact (fan fiction of Ep. 89, "Star Trek: The Next Generation")

Academic
Media Management in the Age of Giants: Business Dynamics of Journalism (1st and 2nd editions of textbook)

Published with Beatrice Herrick
A genealogy book for family members

.

Made in the USA
Coppell, TX
30 January 2024